The Call To Write

An Invitation To Aspiring Writers

Conversation Series

William L. White

Pamela Woll
for Prevention First, Inc.

Library of Congress Cataloging in Publication Data

White, William L., 1947-
   The Call to Write: An invitation to aspiring writers/William L. White,
Pamela Woll.
     p.   cm.
   ISBN 0-938475-05-3
   1. Authorship. I. Woll, Pamela. 1952-   . II. Title.
PN147.W456   1995
808' .02--dc20   95-1777
                                                           CIP

                  Published by the Lighthouse Institute
                          Bloomington, Illinois

Additional copies of this publication may be obtained by sending $12.95 plus
$3.00 shipping and handling to:

                     Lighthouse Institute Publishing
                        702 West Chestnut Street
                     Bloomington, Illinois 61701-2814
                           (309) 827-6026

Other books by William L. White that are available from the Institute include:

- Incest in the Organizational Family: The Ecology of Burnout in Closed
  Systems (1986)
- The Culture of Addiction, The Culture of Recovery (1990)
- Critical Incidents: Ethical Issues in Substance Abuse Prevention and
  Treatment (1993)
- The Training Life: Living and Learning in the Substance Abuse Field (1994)

The Conversation Series

This book is one of a series of books and monographs published by the Lighthouse Institute on areas of specialized skill within the field of behavioral health. Each work in the series engages two or more people in conversation about their areas of special expertise. Like all the works in the series, this one contains personal anecdotes, skill development resources, practical suggestions, career options, and "how-to" guidance—all within the language and tone of a personal conversation.

Dear Friend and Colleague,

All health and human service professionals write. We write client histories. We write up service activities. We write letters, memos and reports. We write policies and procedures. We write plans and grant proposals. And yet some of us aspire to a very different kind of writing.

Do you feel you have perceptions and thoughts that could be of interest or benefit to others? Do you find yourself drawn to the beauty of words? Have you ever read an article or book and thought afterwards, "I could have written that." Are you drawn to stories and the meanings they contain? Do you find yourself doodling words and ideas in response to things going on around you? Have you ever tried and enjoyed writing outside the context of academic or professionally assigned work? Do you have an interest in how writers create their works? Have you ever thought about writing as a medium for personal growth or as a vehicle for service? If so, you may be one of the people we are looking for.

We are looking for aspiring writers, young and old. We are looking for people without writing experience and people who may already be writing and wish to compare their experiences with those of other writers. We are looking for people who are interested in developing and refining their writing skills. If you are such a person, we invite you to join us in a detailed conversation about the writing craft and the writing life. Our motive for this invitation is simple and straightforward. The field needs writers and we want to entice you to help fill this void.

This book is an invitation and an orientation to the process of writing for personal growth and professional service. It explores in detail many aspects of the writing craft and the writer's lifestyle. It discusses diverse writing forms—the journal, the professional article, the research report, the monograph, the book. The two authors, William White and Pamela Woll, have extensive experience writing within and for the substance abuse prevention and treatment fields. Bill is a Senior Research Consultant for the Lighthouse Institute in Bloomington, Illinois. Pam is Senior Writer in the Chicago office of the Illinois Prevention Resource Center, a project of Prevention First, Inc. Both discuss the development of writing skills, the craft of writing, the challenges of writing, and the many kinds of writing they have undertaken in their fields.

This is not a book you have to read cover to cover. Skip and dance your way through, pausing at those areas that catch your interest. We have tried to create the feel of a late-night conversation between friends and colleagues in front of a fireplace—a blend of mutual respect, camaraderie, and warmth. So come join us to discuss the challenges, frustrations, and magic of this call to write. Use our thoughts and experiences to stimulate your own reflections. Ultimately this is a book about you and your potential as a writer.

Bill White
Pam Woll

Acknowledgements

We would like to acknowledge the support of our two agencies, the Lighthouse Institute and Prevention First, Inc., for their recognition of the need for such a product and their willingness to grant time toward its completion.

Deep appreciation goes to the following reviewers who offered many helpful critiques of early drafts: Barbara Allen, Rita Chaney, Rob Furey, Valerie Hoskins, Shirley Pacely, and Michelle Pillen. Technical assistance in preparation of the manuscript was provided by Joyce Thomas.

Table of Contents

Part I: Two Writers

Part II: The Writing Craft

Chapter 7: Readers, Reviewers, Collaborators and Employers

Part III: The Writing Life

Part I

Two Writers

"Fool!" said my muse to me, "look in thy heart, and write."

—Sir Philip Sidney (16th-Century English writer)

Chapter 1

Bill

Pam: First of all, how do you feel about discussing your writing and the craft of writing?

Bill: I feel a sense of anticipation and a tinge of anxiety. The excitement comes from moving into new territory. This will be the first in-depth exploration I've done of my own writing process. My anxiousness springs from uncertainty about how much of my writing psychology is transferable to other writers.

Pam: That makes sense. I've heard that writers and other artists tend to be ambivalent about discussing their craft.

Bill: Some writers talk endlessly about their craft, often achieving a great deal more artistic posturing than writing. Others maintain silence in the superstitious fear that the sources of their creativity might flee in the face of conscious scrutiny. There seems to be something about artistic craft that defies a too-conscious scrutiny. W.C. Fields lost the ability to juggle for six years after he read a scientific analysis of how he performed his act. I share the superstition against analyzing one's craft too rigorously. Besides, the writing process is still such a mystery to me, I'm never sure my explanation of how I write is *really* how I write.

Pam: I think we like the fact that it's a mystery, too. When we were planning these conversations you mentioned that you didn't want to discuss your current writing projects in detail. Is that hesitancy part of this superstition?

Bill: Ernest Hemingway admonished writers never to talk about writing that was in process. He believed that such talk spoiled the freshness of the material and weakened its composition. I think there's some truth to this. Writing is a kind of discovery process for me. If I've thought and talked a subject out, I lose the magic of discovery that energizes the writing process. If the subject has been fully explored in my mind, it's time to go on to new places. The thinking, emoting, and writing must be timed together to achieve the best product. I'll talk in detail about past projects. You'll have to pardon me if I gloss over my current projects.

Pam: Absolutely. Now something has made you want to talk about the process of writing. What is it?

Bill: It has to do with timing—this particular time in my life and this particular time in our field. For me, it has something to do with maturing as a writer. I had to generate a body of work before I could stop and ask how I had created it. A premature self-examination could have jinxed the creative process—there's my superstition showing again. I think such examination today may provide discoveries that can enhance my writing abilities. If it doesn't, I'll be quite disappointed. As a field, we are in a period of tumultuous change. In the midst of such turbulence, it's important that we generate a body of literature that can capture our history and point the way to the future.

Pam: What other personal goals do you have for these conversations?

Bill: I hope to stimulate others' interest in writing. I also think it will be a great opportunity to capture at a particular point in time our thoughts about the writing process and the role of the writer within the behavioral health field. I hope in years to come we can look back over these published interviews with a warm sense of nostalgia and a minimum of embarrassment.

Personal Writing History

Pam: Can you identify your first attraction to writing?

Bill: My first attraction was not to writing—it was a sense of identification with writers' passion for excess. In my earliest introduction to literature, my rural school teachers whispered the various insanities, addictions, obsessions and strange idiosyncracies exhibited so commonly in the great writers. Feeling pretty crazy at that point in my life, I thought I had the natural proclivity for deviance to qualify for potential membership in this club. I just wasn't sure I had any inclination or skill to write.

Pam: Do you think that certain types of developmental experiences are more inclined to produce writers?

Bill: The passion to create is often ignited out of our childhood experiences. Many writers experienced an early sense of alienation and aloneness that sharpened their observational skills and forced them to fill their solitude. As a child, I discovered a special place of sanctuary within the safety of my own mind. The ability to find comfort within my own thoughts, fantasies and images occurred long before I wrote my first words. Developmental pain seems to be a prerequisite for great writing, or at least experiences that in their jolting impact heighten the sensibilities.

I've always felt that I was living on the fringe of this society. In this marginal world of the border, in this self-imposed cultural limbo, I find myself neither in nor out. The answer to the question "Who am I?" is to a very real extent the answer to the question, "What is my relationship with this culture?" As writers, we are always struggling to work out our relationship with the culture in which we find ourselves. It's a mutual ambivalence. The culture isn't sure what to do with us either.

Pam: What role do you think this sense of sanctuary-away-from-others plays in the craft of writing?

Bill: Most of the great writers experience something that separates them from their fellow human beings. They live in a state of psychological exile. They use their detachment as fuel for their art. It's the source of the writer's independence of spirit—their willingness to test boundaries and challenge authority. Writers develop places of inner sanctuary from which they can watch and make sense of the world.

We go down into ourselves or look into the souls of others and then come back and tell the world what we have seen and learned. Each time we go on such a quest, we're not entirely sure of the way back. When writers bring their work to the world, they're like Lazarus rising from the dead, Jonah emerging from the belly of the whale, or Dorothy returning to Kansas.

Pam: That's interesting. Those sound like resurrection images. For every death there's a birth, and for every birth, a death.

When did you actually begin writing?

Bill: I mark the beginning of my writing in my senior year in high school. At the age of 17, I encountered an English teacher who entered our little school system like Don Quixote. He had an instinct for "empowerment" long before the term's discovery and overuse. He simply said, "Think and write." He was more interested in inciting our imaginations than in refining our grammar. He challenged us to find the best way to communicate thoughts that he convinced us were of immense importance.

This was the beginning of my discovery of the sheer pleasure produced by expressing thoughts and feelings on paper. I mark the birth of my writing (and in many ways, my thinking) from this time and the influence of this strange and sensitive man.

Pam: Did you get some training in writing during your college years?

Bill: Not in a direct way. I meandered through college departments, absorbing information from one and then moving on to another. I had no respect for the normal territorial boundaries within which colleges and universities compartmentalize knowledge. I started with the sciences, moved into a divisional major combining religion, philosophy and English, and eventually graduated with a divisional major in psychology, sociology and history. I had no formal writing classes, but did considerable writing and got exposed to great literature across those disciplines. I wish I had found more opportunities for formal training in writing.

Pam: There seems to have been a break in your writing during the early 1970s. Was there?

Bill: Yes, writing during this period simply couldn't compete with the world of work. I was involved in work that was creative, exciting, and personally meaningful. The writing couldn't compete with the intensity of living. By the time college was over, I wanted to throw myself at real problems and challenges. The intensity of street work with addicts and being involved in organizing community mental health and addiction services was very exhilarating. Writing was much too contemplative to feed my appetite for action.

Pam: When did you start to write again?

Bill: In 1976, I went through an intense self-appraisal of my professional future. After nine years in direct service and clinical supervision, I felt stuck. I needed to get out of the addictions field or take a deeper plunge into the field. I finally settled on the latter with two decisions. The first was to pursue a Master's degree in addiction studies. The second was to move to Chicago and get experience working with substance abuse within an urban context. These were important decisions for my professional development and my writing.

The intense intellectual stimulation at Goddard College primed my writing pump once again. My employment with the Illinois Dangerous Drugs Commission and later the Chicago-based training center of the National Institute on Drug Abuse demanded a great deal of professional writing.

Pam: Were you involved in direct delivery of prevention and treatment services at the time?

Bill: Not at first. It was the first time in nine years that I wasn't involved in clinical work, and this posed a problem. As I explored the literature of substance abuse research—material I had never been exposed to in my direct service years—I found myself needing a continued source of face-to-face contact with alcoholics, addicts and community organizations to test many of my new questions and ideas. I was able to resolve this by getting involved with local prevention and treatment agencies on a part time basis.

Pam: So you need to filter your thinking and your writing through direct experience?

Bill: That has been true throughout my writing career. There have been a lot of ideas within the history of the addiction field that looked superficially meaningful but failed the test of utility in the real world. My slant at writing has always been to filter ideas through experience. The ideas are not mature—ready to be written—until I can illustrate them through the experience of real people.

Writing *Incest in the Organizational Family*

Pam: What was it like writing your first book?

Bill: The birthing of that book was a long process. Between 1976 and 1978, I was doing research through my involvement with Goddard College on the process of burnout among workers in human service organizations. My researches lead me to understand the way in which staff burnout was exacerbated by aberrations in group dynamics within organizations. I began applying the literature on enmeshed family systems and the literature on incest, in particular, to a process of organizational closure very common in small human service organizations. I wrote a little paper called "Incest in the Organizational Family: An Initial Inquiry" and sent it to a few people around the country for review.

That paper had a life of its own—it got passed from person to person like an underground document. Its movement across the country began generating speaking and consultation requests. In 1979, I had three monographs published in which I substantially expanded upon the ideas in the initial paper. These monographs generated feedback and consultation requests that brought me a wealth of new experiences in different kinds of organizations.

In response to requests for a more detailed presentation of the ideas presented in the monographs and in my lectures, I wrote the book *Incest in the Organizational Family* during 1985 and published it through the Institute in the Spring of 1986. It's about to go into its fourth printing.

Pam: What's it like to pick up that book and read it today?

Bill: I still feel good about what I had to say in that book, but the writing style would be different today. There is an acute self-consciousness that breathes through its every page. There exists within those pages an ever present awareness of my attempt to write a book. That self-consciousness produced language that was overly formal and constrained. When my writing flowed, I edited it into my mental image of a more "professionally proper" form. My main regret about that book is that I didn't trust my instincts about how to present my message. I was just too unsure of myself. I was confident of the ideas, but unsure of my voice—unsure of myself as a writer. It took a long time to write my way through that self-consciousness.

Pam: Where did that self-consciousness come from?

Bill: Writing a book was such a gigantic leap beyond my own background. The few men on my mother's side of the family who went to college, did so on athletic scholarships, and men on my dad's side didn't graduate from high school, let alone college. The act of writing a book was such a far stretch from those roots. Not having sprung from personal traditions of power, there was a nagging hesitancy to speak—a haunting feeling that I was an impostor in the world of intellectual achievement.

Pam: What might a new writer learn from this experience?

Bill: Many beginning writers will have to fight their own ghosts and learn to defy the voices that taunt them into silence or into an artificial form. You have to shut off the voices that say, "Who do you think you are? You can't do this!" My advice is to be bold and bodacious in your approach to writing. There is a special sense when you are on the writing path that is meant for you—that place each writer must discover and stay tuned to. If what you create from that space is rejected, it's an external rejection—the writer in executing the work has been true to the self.

Ralph Waldo Emerson rightly observed that imitation was suicide. In imitating others, we suffocate our own creative self. If one mimics the style and voice of others, acceptance or rejection by others is a betrayal of oneself. If the mimicked work succeeds, one feels an impostor because the work didn't come from one's true self. If the mimicked work fails, it's a double failure—a failure in courage to reveal one's own voice and a failure in copying the voices of others who are successful.

Writing *The Culture of Addiction, The Culture of Recovery*

Pam: Your second book, *The Culture of Addiction, The Culture of Recovery*, is more than 500 pages long. How long did it take to write?

Bill: It took about a year of concentrated activity but those periods of concentrated writing were scattered over three years. I go through intense periods of training and travel and then try to write during four-to-six-week sabbaticals at home. Most of that book was written during such periods in the summers of 1989 and 1990.

Pam: Do you consider yourself a fast writer?

Bill: When the thinking is going well, the writing can be very fast. I can't write until I have the broad picture of what I'm doing in my head and have a gut feel for how I'm going to express that picture. Getting this cognitive map and instinctive feel for the tone and flavor of what one is about to write can be agonizing. The writing that follows is often a great joy.

Pam: Did the length of *The Culture of Addiction, The Culture of Recovery* make it harder to write?

Bill: No. Writing a long work requires less skill and is less demanding than a short treatment of the same subject. There are fewer demands for synthesis and summation in longer works and the depth of detail makes the longer work much less likely to be misunderstood and misapplied. I've always preferred more expansive writing formats.

The Challenge of Writing *Critical Incidents*

Pam: In the introduction to your book, *Critical Incidents*, you wrote that the book was difficult to write, and that its creation was more work than pleasure. What did you mean by that?

Bill: I don't think I've ever tackled a writing assignment that required such sustained concentration. *Critical Incidents* was a book I felt was desperately needed by the field. Although I wasn't sure I was the best person to do it, I got tired of waiting for someone else to take up the challenge. This book was written out of a sense of love and obligation to the field—a form of re-payment—not out of my expertise or joy for the subject.

Pam: I've heard you say you were a bit overwhelmed by that book. What did you mean?

Bill: The ethical dilemmas presented in the book were experienced over many years. Each dilemma represented risks to real clients, threats to the reputations of real workers and agencies, and potential harm to other parties. I was able to get through those situations by seeing each as an isolated case. In preparing

Critical Incidents I re-experienced these events all at once, and yes, it was a bit overwhelming. In fact, I was concerned that the book would overwhelm readers in a similar manner. I was afraid that confronting the reader with the sheer frequency and complexity of the ethical issues encountered by front-line prevention and treatment specialists would frighten rather than educate and empower.

Pam: I don't know. When people have run into enough ethical problems in their own careers, they begin to get a sense of how widespread the problems really are, even if they push those thoughts aside. It may be that you named some of their fears, but I doubt that you created them. Besides, you gave people some excellent tools for dealing with the problems. I think they came out ahead.

It seems to me that your writing style in *Critical Incidents* is different from that of your earlier books.

Bill: There is a difference in style. My first two books were, in some ways, overwritten. There's a danger in doing too much work for the reader. Writers who over-describe and over-explain reinforce passivity and laziness in their readers. They see their readers as empty vessels to be filled with the author's knowledge. In *Critical Incidents*, I left open spaces for the reader. I didn't answer all the questions, and I tried to avoid simplistic formulas in responding to very complex issues. While some readers may be frustrated by this lack of rule-oriented prescription, I don't think a workable book on ethics within our field could be written in any other way. It was crucial to approach this subject in a way that didn't reinforce the field's propensity for closed, either-or thinking.

Pam: The idea of writing a book on ethics would frighten me. Did it scare you at all?

Bill: I was concerned about whether the field was ready for the kind of book I had in mind and what the personal response would be to my having written such a work. I was concerned about the arrogance that might be attributed to any person who would choose to write about ethical issues. In the current cultural climate, to raise the banner of ethical inquiry is to invite scrutiny and attack. I had the initial feeling that I didn't have the expertise or moral authority to write such a book. That feeling slowed for a considerable period my decision to initiate work on the book. I finally decided—in fact, was told by others—that

I was ducking an opportunity for service to the field because of my own petty fears and insecurities. There was a growing sense that if moral perfection was a requirement for authorship, the book would never be written by anyone.

Pam: And if anyone volunteered to write it, watch out for them!

Bill: Yes! But it was at that point that I felt a growing sense of duty to begin work on *Critical Incidents*. The book emerged, not out of courage, but out of a confrontation with my own insecurity.

The Conversation Series

Pam: Your fourth book, *The Training Life*, involved collaborators and introduced a new writing format for you. What attracted you to the idea of "conversations on paper?"

Bill: For years people who have attended my workshops have asked questions about such areas as writing, training, and consultation. I thought it would be a great format to collapse those many questions into flowing interviews on various specialty skill areas within the field. I also wanted to experiment with the style of writing in which people with specialized expertise talked conversationally to the reader.

Working on *The Training Life* was a joy not only because of the pleasure of working with Bruce Joleaud, Felicia Dudek and Bob Carty and my passion for the topic, but also because of my desire to begin to experiment with the kind of "conversation on paper" reflected in this book. I thought such a format might have great appeal to a field with such strong oral traditions. In form, I wanted to find an artistic synthesis of the book, the advice column, the letter, the interview, and the conversation.

The challenge was to write something that had the warmth and informality of a transcribed conversation. You can never just transcribe a conversation, because they rarely make sense on paper. So much meaning is lost when the nuances of gesture and tone are reduced to words on paper and removed from the context of time, place, and relationship. To create on paper what feels like a conversation is a technical writing achievement that can rarely if ever be achieved through the simple act of transcribing. I wanted to create through the reader's eyes what all the senses experience in human conversation.

Pam: How did you approach those challenges?

Bill: I experimented with soliciting questions and writing responses; I taped, transcribed and edited interviews; and I experimented with writing condensed topical observations in a conversational format. The trick was to delete all the rambling and repetition found in normal speech, while maintaining detail and flow and feeling.

Overview of Writing Career

Pam: What's your assessment of yourself as a writer today?

Bill: I'm probably a better thinker than writer. My desire to improve my writing is driven by my desire to more articulately express my thinking. I often feel frustrated that my skills of language are not adequate to the challenge of expressing the ideas I'm trying to communicate. I still struggle in my effort to produce writing that is both personal and powerful.

Many writers have talked about the importance of voice in writing. Voice is like a signature or fingerprint of the writer. I think my best writing has always closely approximated my speaking voice. It's this voice in my writing that maintains consciousness of words as vehicles of communication. It's a directness, an intensity and a pitch that mirrors my training voice. My worst writing displays words from inside my head that are not directed to anyone.

Pam: I know what you mean. It's that self-consciousness that you mentioned earlier. What other challenges do you face as a writer?

Bill: There are still basics of the writing craft I'm struggling to master. I make errors in basic diction and grammar that I feel like I should have mastered by now. I still struggle with the need for brevity and clarity. I tend to have five writing projects going, while resisting bringing any to final completion. Perhaps another weakness is that my writing tends to be serious in its subject matter and emotionally intense in its tone. I'm working on how to more effectively integrate a wider range of emotional experience within my writing. In my training, I've found ways to structure an ebb and flow of intensity so I don't wear the trainee out. I'm still searching for the skills to create this ebb and flow in my writing.

Pam: Are there recurring themes in your writing?

Bill: The most central theme is probably that of change. My writing focuses to a great extent on the need and potential for transformation of individuals, organizations, and whole cultures. Much of my work begins with an exploration of pain and conflict and then attempts to explore sources of hope and reconciliation. I think the resolution of tension and conflict are at the core of great writing.

Another central theme is that of service. The four central activities of my life: counseling, training, consulting, and writing are all acts of service. What I'm doing when I write is giving. Focusing on writing as an act of service helps temper the artistic propensity for self-indulgence and narcissism.

Pam: Do you regret anything that you've written—anything you'd call back today if you could?

Bill: I regret one word. I wish in my first book I would have substituted the word "incestuous" for the word "incest." If I had used the word incestuous, it would have been more clear that I was using incest as an analogy and a metaphor. By coining the term "organizational incest," I risked diluting the meaning of the word incest and disrespecting the unique experiences of incest survivors.

Only one person has written to express objection to my use of this term in the fifteen years since my early writing on closed systems, but it's an issue that I've given considerable thought to over the last several years. If a new edition of my first book is ever released, there will be references to incestuous dynamics within organizations but I will delete the phrases "organizational incest" and "incest in the organizational family." Saying something has similarities to incest is very different than saying something is incest. We must take responsibility for how our inventions—our ideas and metaphors—can be used and abused.

Pam: That almost implies a separate stage of reviewing, where we'd go over what we've written in a very literal-minded way, and think of all the ways it might be taken. I like that idea.

Motivation to Write

Pam: We've talked about some of your major writing activities. Let me ask you a more basic question: Why write? What motivates you, and what do you believe motivates other writers—particularly in this field?

Bill: The passion to write is so personal that I suspect it springs from different sources for each writer and from many sources within the same writer. My writing is primarily a search for understanding and meaning. It's a response to joy and suffering.

My most significant writing projects, my books, I think spring from the discomfort of anger or impatience. Some psychologists think all creativity is an attempt to resolve conflict. My first book, *Incest in the Organizational Family*, was unquestionably such an attempt. After watching several wonderful organizations evolve into near self-destruction, I tried to discover what had happened. The book summarized the answers to that question and sounded a call of warning to others about the dangers of closed organizational systems.

The passion to write often comes to me when I feel otherwise powerless in the face of some injustice. Writing is my antidote to powerlessness. It counteracts my sense of helplessness when other areas of action are not possible. I've always experienced writing as a subversive act, as an act of resistance. I still believe in the power of the written word to inspire hope, heal individuals, and transform the world, and I must confess some embarrassment with that belief. Part of me views this belief as incredibly naive, and yet I continue to believe. Perhaps faith is a more appropriate word.

Pam: I don't think it's naive. We've all experienced transformation in our individual lives, and seen examples of it in the world at large. I mean, we can just sit here and complain, or we can try something.

Bill: That's just it. For years I sat on the sidelines judging my field while refusing to risk involvement in the forums which shaped the field. There comes a time when you have to give up the safe role of the armchair critic and enter fully into the professional dialogue of your chosen field. You enter that dialogue through the channels the field has created to conduct its discourse. It's this conversation that shapes the world in which you work. You can't influence this world if you can't get in the conversation. You must discover your voice and seek out forums where this voice can be heard. Writing is one way of finding your voice and getting published is one way to be heard.

I think what writers are ultimately struggling to achieve is a definition of the big picture, to tell THE story behind the little stories. Young writers can sometimes catch this big picture through the freshness of their vision; seasoned writers discover the big picture through slow revelations of the tissue that connects a lifetime of little stories.

Pam: I like that image. A simple and straightforward little story is rarely just simple and straightforward.

Bill: When one has spent a lifetime listening to people reveal themselves one layer at a time, it becomes clear that the shared story both reveals and conceals. Like the layers of an onion, each new story reveals the story hidden by the previous story and hides the story yet to be exposed.   The story is thus simultaneously a window and a shroud; that's what makes them so wonderfully engaging. E.B. White once said that writing was both a mask and an unveiling. It took me a long time to understand the meaning of his words.

Pam: This places a significant responsibility on the writer to portray the "wholeness" of the story. What happens if we don't do it accurately?

Bill: Where we lack precision in our thinking and writing, we contribute to the perpetuation of a problem; we increase the likelihood of misdiagnosis and inappropriate intervention. Many problems are not at all what we have defined them to be. I recently read an analysis of 1990 census data prepared by the noted demographer Harold Hodgkinson. He contends that much of what we attribute to race in this culture is really a phenomenon of economic class. By focusing exclusively on race and racism, we may miss the broader story of the economic restructuring of this country.

There is a tendency to tell a story from a simple slant in a form short enough for rapid consumption by the reader. Few problems can ever be defined with such simplicity. The ability to capture and elucidate complexity is an essential art for the 21st century writer. There is a circularity and interconnectedness of our current problems that defies compartmentalization and simplistic solutions. We must strive to tell the big stories out of which our little stories flow. We must strive to tell how our individual stories influence the big picture. If we tell only either, we lie by omission.

Pam: Yes. And if we tell both, we risk losing the readers who want to hear something more simplistic, or something that they already agree with. What other motivations have you noticed in yourself?

Bill: I suppose I write out of a desire for recognition and immortality. I write because it's cheaper and easier than therapy. I often write to experience the pleasure of the muses and vanquish the demons of the creative process. I write to defy the whispers inside my head that admonish me to remain silent. I also write a lot to find out what is inside me. Writers always seem to be describing writing as a process of discovery. It's exactly that for me. I sit down and write to discover what I think about something—I often don't know what I think until the moment I write it. I'm surprised that—even with writing about subjects that I believe I've thought out long before I begin composing—there are always invisible shadows of my experience with a subject that are only revealed through the act of writing.

Pam: Do you ever write in anger?

Bill: I get angry and struggle against systems and myself. Writing is a way for me to fight the Goliaths, and it's a way for me to confront my own ignorance. There is an undercurrent of love in most of this anger. I can be angry at this country because I also love it. I can express outrage at the field because I love it and wish to protect and nurture its future. I can be angry at myself because I know I'm capable of better.

Pam: Do your emotions ever change during the writing process? Do you ever begin a work driven by one emotion, and end up with a different emotional attitude and atmosphere?

Bill: As you release an emotion into the writing process, it often turns to something else. I began writing *Incest in the Organizational Family* in anger but I reached a stage of playfulness in which I delighted in the realization that this book would put a giant fly in the field's soup. It was a recognition that people would read this book and never again look at organizations in the same way. There was a childlike impishness in my first realization of the writer's power.

Pam: I guess that's something every writer has to come to terms with. If we don't acknowledge that we like the sense of power, we're much more likely to abuse it.

Do you find yourself doing things to nurture your motivation to write?

Bill: I don't believe the creative zeal can be artificially developed, but I think you have to create and protect the circumstances under which the urge to write will flourish. A musician once told Shelby Foote: "What you need to write blues is no money in the bank and nobody loving you." Foote said that when he heard this he felt an obligation to get rid of his money and alienate people so he wouldn't be either rich or loved. It's amazing what some of us are tempted to do for the sake of this passion to write.

Pam: Hmmm let's hope the **memory** of having no money in the bank and nobody loving you would be enough.

Do you think the motivation to write changes in mid- or late-career?

Bill: As you create a body of work, there is an internal demand to keep moving into new territory, breaking new barriers, going beyond what one did the last time. I have a compulsive need to jump into new territory. I think it's a fear that the success of one of my books will trap me within its covers and take years to write my way out of.

Influence of Family, Culture and Place

Pam: Did your family play a supportive role in your writing?

Bill: I'm deeply indebted to my family's support for much of what I've achieved in my professional life. I have vivid childhood memories of writing at the kitchen table, smells of my mother's cooking permeating the room, knowing she would be there later to read and appreciate what I was writing. I think my mom could have been a writer. She had beautiful handwriting and was always copying down poems and phrases she liked or writing down little anecdotes. In contrast, I've never in my life seen my father write anything other than his name. "Pappy" had less than a sixth-grade education and provided a different and less direct support to my writing. He encouraged my education, I think knowing that my every advancement would widen the gap between our experience and our worlds. He could have selfishly constrained me, but he didn't. To the best of my knowledge, he's never read one of my books, but I think it means something to him that I've written them. My tribe of siblings — blood, adopted and foster — always listened, encouraged, applauded, and challenged me. One of my sisters, Shirley Pacely, is a published poet.

Pam: In a rural setting like that, were there ever any cultural forces that tried to discourage boys or men from writing?

Bill: There were early on. In the world of blue collar workers in which I was raised, there seemed something distinctly unmasculine about the act of writing. It had these peculiar associations with "queerness," madness, and drunkenness, only the last of which was generally acceptable. In a world awash in sweat and testosterone, writing seemed too introspective and too directly connected to the world of ideas and emotions.

Pam: How did you deal with that?

Bill: There were countervailing forces. There was pressure to be part of that working class culture, but at the same time there were pressures to move beyond it. My folks wanted me to be comfortable in our world at the same time they wanted me to rise above it. The encouragement to rise above included encouragement for my early literary experiments.

Pam: What about place? Has there been an influence of place on your thinking and writing?

Bill: Perhaps. I was raised in a small village of less than 300 people where one knew and was known by everyone. There was a sense of "hickness" that had to be shed—a need to prove myself in large schools, large agencies, and large cities.   It took some time to understand the special gifts my rural background had bestowed upon me. I had grown up watching the interactions of a small dynamic system and came to learn that there were commonalities in all systems—that Chicago and Washington D.C. were just large villages, that my historical experience had universal validity. I'm like Agatha Christe's Miss Marple, who solved the most complex crimes based on the knowledge and experience she gained in St. Mary Meade. I developed a confidence that I could use elements of my experience in this small arena to navigate my way through the whole world.

Pam: Did this confidence and excitement about writing carry into your college years?

Bill: I wish I could claim some great artistic vision for my college writing, but the honest answer is that much of my writing in college was motivated by my need for money. I made it through college scraping together scholarships, fellowships, and jobs both on and off the campus. I discovered that one of the fastest ways I could make money was writing papers for other students whose financial resources were more plentiful than either their brains or their inclination for academic work. I must confess that my need for money suppressed the ethical qualms I had about such activity. I had to be somewhat careful conducting this enterprise on a small campus. On more than one occasion I had a faculty member with whom I was not taking a course tell me with pointed humor that they enjoyed my paper on such and such—a paper recently submitted in their class under another student's name. I entered literary contests for much the same reasons: the offer of cash prizes for the winners.

In my early college years I actually lost some of my excitement for writing through exposure to teachers who cared more about dangling participles than ideas. I experimented with different types of writing and won a few prizes in literary contests for essays and short stories. In my junior year, I discovered writing as a tool of protest, and used my classes as an excuse to launch into lengthy writing projects through which I explored my own thinking about issues that were important to me.   My personal writing—short fiction, essays, a play—also focused on political and social issues of the day.

Pam: You mentioned the teachers who cared more about the mechanics of writing than its purpose and content. Do you think that's why many people's experiences with writing are so negative?

Bill: Most of our writing efforts are punished rather than affirmed. Traditional models of teaching writing teach us to become fixated on mistakes. What gets modeled to us by our teachers is the art of criticism. This modeling makes us ruthless critics—we become so self-critical, we see ourselves as incapable of writing. This approach snuffs out the creative fires of many would-be writers. The writing self is created long before the first words ever appear on paper. Many budding artists are wounded at this early stage of development and can never fully create until these wounds are healed.

Pam: How do people go about getting those wounds healed?

Bill: For some, the wounds are never healed. Their awareness of the creative spirit within them has been vanquished or, even when such awareness exists, they are not willing to risk its exposure. For others, healing occurs through time, self-discovery and the experience of empowering relationships—people who incite our imaginations and affirm our productive capabilities. Cultivation of this spirit is as essential as training in the writing craft.

Pam: We have talked about the influence of culture and place on the writer. What about the influence of time?

Bill: Every work is rooted in time, and yet some books have the ability to transcend these roots. Each of my books was grounded at a particular time of my life and a particular period of development of the field. A writer could never again write the same book. You write out of a physical and psychological condition and a social environment that is constantly changing. There's a synergy of temperament and circumstance that shapes the character of each work in a way that could never again be exactly replicated.

Current Projects and Future Plans

Pam: Would you ever like to write full time?

Bill: I would like to increase my writing time, but I don't think I could write exclusively.   My writing is so energized by my other involvements in the field—my research, training and consulting activities—it's hard to imagine writing without these sources of stimulation. It probably has something to do with how I learn. I don't care how much reading I do on a subject, I can't write it until I filter it through my experience. By interviewing clients and service providers as part of my research activities, I can perform reality checks on how I'm perceiving and thinking about critical issues within the field.

Pam: What writing projects are you working on now?

Bill: At the Institute, we're sketching out the remainder of the "Conversation Series" of books and working on a series of monographs. Most of my recent writing effort has been directed toward finishing the book *Voices of Survival, Voices of Service*. It's the story of the AIDS Foundation of Chicago's model of AIDS case management.

Pam: What projects are you planning for the future?

Bill: I have several book projects underway but I hope to complete a number of smaller monographs before casting all my energies back into the books.

Pam: What do you hope to accomplish by the end of your writing career?

Bill: My literary agenda is to make a contribution across the breadth of the field in such areas as history, social policy, organizational health, ethics, pharmacology, special populations, treatment philosophy and technique, and prevention. In the process of making this contribution, I hope to recruit and inspire a new generation of trainers and writers to whom I may pass my professional torch.

I sometimes wonder how the pieces of what I create will fit together. It's like each completed work is a piece in an unknown jigsaw puzzle. It's only when my life's work nears completion that I will likely be able to read the story portrayed by the individual pieces. I look forward to the revelation of this picture—to look back and say, "So that's what my life was really about."

Pam: Are you interested in exploring any other forms of writing at this point in your life?

Bill: I've been drawn to poetry in this last year because I have encountered experiences of such intensity that my prose doesn't adequately capture their essence. Writing poetry lets me experience the emotional side of those issues I wrestle with intellectually in my non-fiction work.

Pam: Do you think you'll ever write a major work of fiction?

Bill: I may if I live long enough. I've been making notes for many years on a novel that incorporates my understanding of addiction and recovery. We need all kinds of writers in the field. We need technical writers, journalists, essayists, authors of our professional and self-help books, but we also need novelists and poets and playwrights.

Pam: I couldn't agree more. Even the best piece of non-fiction in the addictions or prevention field stands very little chance of being noticed or read in the "world at large"—among people who may have the greatest need for increased awareness and understanding of these issues. If public awareness is being raised at all, a lot of that is probably due to fiction, movies, and biographies of famous people. We need stories to help us feel and understand things. It's almost as if something has to look like fiction before we can believe it.

You seem to have found something very special in your long-time involvement in the addictions field. What is it?

Bill: I've carried on a 27-year love affair with this field. I've received so much and experienced so much that it's hard to isolate the elements. Perhaps one of the most personal things I've found is an organizing metaphor for my own life. I've come to view addiction and recovery as metaphors for the rhythms and cycles of life: from death comes rebirth, the growing snake sheds its skin, the grotesque caterpillar becomes the butterfly of uncommon beauty. I've found in my professional work what is to me the ultimate miracle of life: this capacity for transformation and growth.

Pam: What do you wish for yourself in the coming years?

Bill: I want to live as fully as I can, contribute as fully as I can, and rest and reflect. Then I want to kiss death on the lips and leave with a smile on my face.

Pam: Do you feel any sort of master plan that's been guiding your career moves and writing projects?

Bill: My career is marked by moving into an area of specialty, absorbing a span of knowledge and skill, and then moving on to a new area. These shifts can be tracked by position changes within agencies and by the ease with which I moved from organization to organization. When I look over my professional life I'm struck by a sense of order and sequence that did not exist as a conscious intent on my part. It's as if each step prepared me for the next. It's as if all of those activities have prepared me for something yet to come. Joseph Campbell often noted in his writings and lectures that this sense of order would emerge if one adhered to the admonition: "Follow your bliss." This has been true in my life.

Chapter 2

Pam

Bill: Let's shift the focus over to you. To begin with, how do you feel about discussing your writing, and some of the ways in which it's developed in your life?

Pam: I'm looking forward to it. I'm really grateful to you for asking me to take part in this dialogue. I'm looking forward to comparing and contrasting our creative processes.

Early Writing Experience

Bill: When did you first start to see yourself as a writer?

Pam: That would have been in sixth grade. We had some visiting instructors in to talk about poetry, and each kid in the class wrote a poem. They made a big fuss about my poem—which was a very conventional one, but it had a consistent meter and rhyme scheme, and a logical progression, and used a lot of imagery. I'd never tried writing a poem before, so I just imitated the traditional poetry I'd read. I felt a sense of wonder and joy at their reaction to it, as if somehow being a poet might justify my being so weird.

Bill: Did that encourage you to write more?

Pam: It did at first. I kept a little red notebook in my desk and kept sneaking it out and writing poetry. I carried it with me all the time. It gave life a sense of magic for me—until it got confiscated by the authorities!

I went to a grammar school run by old-style nuns, the ones with the vow of silence and the wooden rulers. (I know several nuns now, and they're wonderful people—worlds away from the ones who taught us.) Those nuns didn't seem very comfortable with me, because my desk was really messy and I was the kind of kid they tended to label "too sensitive." They did scare the grammar into me, though. Now the kid who sat in front of me was named Patricia, and she was always nosing around in my desk when I wasn't there. So one afternoon when I was leaving the classroom to take part in some kind of activity, I put a big note inside my desk: "Get Out, Nosy Patricia!!!"

Unfortunately, the teacher's name was Sister Mary Patricia. Apparently she'd been walking up and down the aisles and she spotted a scrap of paper hanging out of my desk. She opened it up, saw the note and went berserk. Everything that wasn't a textbook got thrown away, including my little red notebook. I don't think I wrote any more until I got safely into the public school system the following year.

Writing Influences

Bill: Did the skills that you learned as a child writing poetry translate into the development of your expository writing skills?

Pam: Definitely. I think I internalized a sense of rhythm and cadence that comes out now in my writing—whenever I don't interfere with it. And imagery and metaphor have also been important to me in most of the kinds of writing I've done. I think doing all those things in a form as concentrated as poetry sort of makes them second nature, so eventually they happen without conscious effort.

Of course, in expository writing all those elements have to be balanced very carefully with what I'm trying to say, and the words that communicate that most clearly and precisely. In learning how to choose words, I'd have to say my mother helped me more than anyone else.

Bill: Is she a writer?

Pam: She's an attorney, so I guess that means she's a writer and a talker—but most of all an arguer! I remember one weekend when I was in high school, and I was writing a paper at home. I kept bugging her, asking her what words would be the best ones to use to say this or that, and she would respond by asking me questions. These were logical questions, aimed at cutting through all the fancy words and shadings of meaning, to find out in direct words what I was trying to say. Then we'd look at all the available words, and find the one that most accurately represented that meaning.

I don't remember the questions, or my answers, but somehow during that weekend I internalized that process of asking and answering questions about what it was I was really trying to say. Now it's so automatic that I'm not even conscious of it as it happens, but I'm convinced that a good course in writing would start by spending a long time on learning to ask and answer questions.

Bill: You majored in creative writing during your first few years at college. Did you foresee yourself doing what you're doing now?

Pam: I didn't foresee anything that ended up happening. I had no idea the prevention field existed, or the treatment field—or the whole not-for-profit world, for that matter. I knew I wanted to help people, but the only suggestions anybody could come up with were "why not be a social worker?" or "how about clinical psychology?" That would have eaten me alive at the time, and somehow I knew it even then. I lacked the sense of detachment-with-love necessary to survive in those professions.

I had this crazy idea that I had to find the "best" possible way to help people—preferably the greatest number of people. Don't get me wrong: I think it was important that I knew I wanted to be of service, but this insistence on finding the **best** way to do that just spun my energies around in a million directions.

Most people in their late teens and early 20s are going through an enormous transition period. I don't see how anybody at that age can know what kind of career they might want for their lives. I've always admired people who did know, but I didn't. I always liked to write, though—poetry, plays, fiction, whatever. Creative writing as a major seemed to offer more freedom than anything else. It also gave me a good excuse to have adventures: I had to have things to write about!

Experience in Journalism

Bill: How did you end up in journalism?

Pam: I took some time off from school, supposedly to have some "life experiences" that I could write about. Well, one of those life experiences was a job on the Galesburg Register-Mail, writing obituaries. In my spare time I wrote obituaries for my friends, killing them off in all sorts of creative ways. That job was pretty short-lived but I enjoyed it. Later, when I got tired of sub-minimum wage and thought about going back to school, I decided to major in journalism. For a while I could convince myself that might be the "best" way to have a positive influence.

Bill: Did the journalism training have some tangible effects on your writing?

Pam: Yes. First, they insisted that everyone in the journalism program take a logic course that combined propositional calculus—symbolic logic—with critical thinking skills. I loved it. I think that's the best grounding a writer can possibly have, essential for anyone who wants to be persuasive, or even just describe things accurately. Life is very complicated, and skills in logic help clarify much of that.

Don't get me wrong: I strongly believe that logic is not enough, and that the most important aspects of life sometimes transcend logic. But there's a big difference between transcending something and simply ignoring it. Unless we have that basic grounding—that understanding and mastery of logical principles—we're going to spend a lot of time and energy crashing into them.

The journalism training itself also focused on a lot of important things: how to catch people's attention and hold it, how to anticipate people's questions and get answers to them, the importance of getting the facts straight, the importance of making things understandable—and, of course, the importance of stories. I think those are all essential priorities in any form of writing. It helped me learn to write quickly and more simply, and use smaller words and shorter sentences. Since I've been away from journalism my sentences have grown out a little bit—and my writing pace has slowed down somewhat—but I'm still conscious of the need for clarity and brevity. It's the brevity part that gives me the most trouble: I still tend to write long, and to be kind of a perfectionist about it.

Bill: After you'd graduated, you worked on a newspaper for a while. Did that turn out to be what you'd expected?

Pam: I worked for a chain of weekly newspapers, covering news and feature stories in four Chicago suburban communities. It was a lot of fun, because I was covering all types of stories and seeing my name in print each week. I had a number of chances to make a real contribution, to really do something worthwhile.

But my forte turned out to be stories about people—just regular people who did unusual things and happened to live in the communities I covered. It was as if I were still writing fiction. I had to stay within the constraints of the information that people gave me, but I was building characters based on my perceptions of them as people. Whether those perceptions were accurate or not I'll never know, but the portraits were positive enough that nobody complained.

I did some other fun things too: I was a garbage man for a day—I'm not sure what the politically correct term for that is these days—and wrote a long feature about it. I also rode in a helicopter for an afternoon, and a police car for a night, and covered a murder trial and an election. So I had some adventures in that job.

Bill: You worked in journalism only a little more than a year. Why did you decide to get out so soon?

Pam: There were a number of reasons. First the rational ones: In general, I believed—and still believe—more in people's right to privacy than in "the people's right to know." If it's a question of public safety or abuse of the public trust, that's one thing. But if we're just probing into someone's life because the public is curious about it, that's quite another thing. I also grew more and more conscious of how easy it would be to make one small mistake and hurt some innocent person's reputation, or put people in danger. I was acutely aware of how easy it is for me to make mistakes, and I think I was afraid of that possibility. I was also bored with a lot of the types of things I had to write about—village board meetings, school board meetings, zoning issues. Those things got old pretty quickly.

A Writer in Search of a Field

Bill: If those were the rational reasons, what about the irrational ones?

Pam: I was pretty crazy. Who was it that said "The unexamined life is not worth leading?" Well, at the time, I had no appropriate tools with which to examine my life. One day I was brushing my teeth and I came up with a song, just like that. It had been years since I'd tried that—writing a song, that is—but the song came out whole. Then I wrote another one a few weeks later. Then another one. It occurred to me that some of my most important insights had come from listening to other people's songs, so maybe my "best" contribution in life might be as a songwriter. Then I went to a songwriters' workshop, and they talked about how easy it is to write hit songs and live off the royalties and just run around the rest of the time having adventures. That was what I wanted to hear!

I spent the next several years working in jobs I didn't like and wasn't well suited for, just hoping that the dissatisfaction would force me to write some of those hit songs so I could live off the royalties. I started off by putting up aluminum siding, then worked for this weird photography company, then a restaurant, then two detective agencies. Part of my work for the detective agencies was writing their reports to clients, but a lot of what I did was purely secretarial. That got me into the trap of being considered only for secretarial jobs—even though I lacked a lot of the concrete skills that were necessary to do those jobs well, but had a lot of more abstract skills that I wasn't considered qualified to use.

Bill: Did your dissatisfaction with these jobs increase your productivity as a writer?

Pam: Of course not. Dissatisfaction isn't what does it: discipline is—or at least it's one of the essential ingredients. Some people become more disciplined as a result of their dissatisfaction with their circumstances, but others just become paralyzed in terms of their confidence and initiative. I was one of those people. The songwriting kind of sputtered and died after a couple of years, partly because I didn't play an instrument so I had no vehicle for developing the musical end of it, and partly because I was putting pressure on the songwriting to be commercially successful. It couldn't develop naturally, so it stopped. It was smarter than I was.

Bill: Did you ever think of going back to journalism?

Pam: I feared going back to journalism. I think my instincts were right, that I really didn't belong there. I just didn't know where I did belong, because I was looking for some perfect way to make a contribution.

Bill: What did those experiences teach you about writing?

Pam: For one thing, they taught me that my purpose for writing has to be at least roughly in line with my overall sense of purpose, or else the process will get distorted and stop. I think that's true of any form of creativity. Now if my overall sense of purpose had to do with money, I'd probably have kept on trying to write hit songs. But it didn't, so I stopped being able to try.

On the other hand, about 10 years ago a series of unlikely coincidences led me to find and begin playing the Celtic harp. My music, which had stopped completely by then, started up again, unrestricted. I learned to play the harp and compose songs on it simply because I knew it was my instrument. I knew it could express the music that went deepest in me better than any other instrument I'd heard. Whether or not that music was commercially viable didn't matter. As a result, I'm still playing, and people want to hear it. I haven't distorted the craft to meet a particular market, the way I tried to distort it when I was writing would-be hit songs. That's an important thing to keep in mind as I move through all the phases of my writing career.

My other major lesson had to do with the importance of having faith in people's abilities, even when their abilities are buried under their circumstances. Those circumstances might include a lack of direction or knowledge or experience, a disability, obstacles they've encountered because of gender or racial or cultural factors—or whatever. During those years after I left journalism, it was almost impossible to get anyone to take my writing or professional potential seriously. I'd been stereotyped as an administrative assistant, and that was how most of the people I worked for saw me.

Bill: So you had an experience of having people fail to believe in you?

Pam: Yes. Many people liked me and said nice things about the work I was doing. But that's different from giving someone a chance to do something more difficult. I felt so trapped for so many years, and there were four people in particular who believed in me during that period. They're still major heroes for me: John Brady, who gave me a chance to really use my brain when I worked for him; Liz Cifani, who told me I had potential on the harp before I'd even learned how to play; the late Sam Hill, my choir director at St. Paul's, who asked me to bring the harp in one Sunday when I'd only been playing about six months and he'd never heard me; and Virginia Martinez, who backed me in my attempt to break out of the secretarial mold and take on a writing project at Voices for Illinois Children.

It takes a lot of courage to believe in people's potential when there's conflicting evidence. We're all so afraid of being wrong, of being made to look like fools. But I think it's better to stand up for people's right to try, even if we end up looking foolish once in a while. The alternative is the waste of a lot of human spirit, talent, ideas and intellect. There are some extraordinary people walking around out there under some very ordinary—or very troubled—exteriors. I think part of my job as a writer is to keep painting that picture, and to look for and encourage the extraordinary in the people around me.

And finally, I learned some excellent lessons about professionalism, and how to respond to professional rejection. Even if I'm not suited for a job or a project, even if it's not using what I believe are my most important skills and talents, it's still the job that's in front of me right now. If I do it—not perfectly—but with care and dignity, I'll be sending a message to others, and to my own mind and emotions, that I respect my work and I respect myself. I used to feel—and undoubtedly look—crushed and hopeless and resentful when I was turned down for a job or a project. Finally I learned to say in a friendly, matter-of-fact way, "Thanks for letting me try. Unless you have any objections, I'll try again the next time something opens up." Eventually, it worked.

Becoming a Professional Writer

Bill: How did it feel when you finally had a chance to start writing again professionally?

Pam: I was elated at first. I remember when I'd just found out that Voices was going to let me quit my administrative assistance position and take on two writing projects as a consultant. I left the office for a minute and went out into the hallway, and my arms just floated up in the air on their own, like wings.

When the work actually started on the projects, I was terrified. I'd done quite a bit of technical writing during the past six years, but these new projects were things that really mattered to me. One was a report on state-funded preschool programs for "children at risk of academic failure," and the other was the result of a statewide conference and focus group process, on early intervention for "young children at risk of developmental delay and disability."

I didn't know if I was smart enough, or good enough, or professional enough. I knew I didn't know enough—at least not at first. For a while every complication I hit would paralyze me, until I was able to identify the fear, or the confusion, or the missing information, or the difference of opinion, or the shift in focus that had caused the blockage. I usually tried to figure it all out by myself for a while, but finally ended up asking for help. Of course asking for help always led to immense relief. We just aren't designed to do it all by ourselves.

By the time I'd almost finished those projects—*Building at the Frontier: Policy Choices for Young Children at Risk*; and (as co-author with Malcolm Bush) *All Our Children Can Make the Grade: A Report on the Illinois Preschool System, Children at Risk of Academic Failure*—I had enough nerve to start circling the substance abuse prevention field and looking for a place to land.

Discovering Prevention

Bill: What were you hoping to do in prevention?

Pam: There were some important concepts that I didn't see being used in prevention, at least not in any central way. For example, a lot of the principles that people encounter in recovery programs—things that often turn out to be very central to success in those programs—didn't seem to be communicated or explored in the prevention efforts that I'd heard about. I'm talking about concepts like forgiveness, teachability, honesty with oneself, healthy interdependence, faith and trust, the intrinsic worth of all people, effective ways of dealing with the illusion of control, and so on.

I always like to start at the center of things, and it seemed to me that the drug information and refusal skills that were the backbone of traditional prevention programs didn't come close to the **center** of the pain and fear that so often lead to abuse, addiction and the full constellation of other problems that surround them. I'd seen kids chanting "just say no" whose family lives and communities were so devastated—and whose inner sense of pain and powerlessness was so deep—that no mere physical or intellectual activity could ever touch it, much less counteract its potential effects. I knew the prevention field had grown past "just say no," but I wanted to find out just how far it was willing to grow, and join forces with the people who were promoting that growth. I didn't know who I was looking for, but I new **what** I was looking for.

Bill: It can be hard approaching an unfamiliar field. Where did you start?

Pam: At the center. I've seldom sent out resumes or had much luck with newspaper want ads. I've always found it more useful to figure out what seems like the central point to do what I want to do, then just approach the central person. Instead of asking, "do you have a job?"—to which the logical answer is "no"—I just say "I'm new to the field and I have some ideas, and I'd like to learn more." Then when I get an appointment, I hit 'em with my writing samples.

I called people until I found out who funded prevention programs. Then I called DASA, the Illinois Department of Alcoholism and Substance Abuse, and hauled my samples over there. DASA didn't have an opening, but it just happened that the Prevention Resource Center (PRC) was about to convert its training resource materials into training manual form, and needed somebody to edit them and get them camera ready. I was referred to PRC's executive director, Jackie Garner, and I came on as a PRC consultant for six months, beginning in January of 1990. It turned out that I fit in perfectly with the organizational culture and mission. At the end of six months they offered me a permanent position.

Bill: You seem pretty happy with your position at PRC/Prevention First. Has it given you a chance to do what you wanted to do?

Pam: Yes, and it's also expanded my view of what I want to do. There are people at PRC/Prevention First with vision and courage, and they're really willing to take chances and try new things. That's been their history. On several occasions they've put everything on the line in order to improve the quality of their services, and it's worked. I needed to find people who would not only have faith in me and take my ideas seriously, but also teach me a lot, and be patient with me while I grew. I found it, and I'm really grateful.

Bill: You mentioned that you came into the field with some points that you wanted to get across.

Pam: Yes. I had a desire to see prevention programs aimed more squarely at the pain and fear that children experience. That desire was given one outlet pretty early in the process. They let me attend the 1990 joint conference of the Illinois Institute on Drugs and Alcohol and the National Association for Children of Alcoholics. I was able to synthesize information from conference sessions into a long *Prevention Forum* article on making all prevention programs more responsive to the needs of all children—including children of addicted families. A year later we expanded those concepts into a manual called *Breaking the Chain*, with Cathleen Brooks serving as Guest Editor. Cathleen is the founder of Next Step, and a pioneer in the COA field.

Bill: What was it like working with Cathleen?

Pam: She was a real joy to work with. She taught me a lot of things, but I guess the most significant was that children's survival systems—like denial, lack of trust, and all those other supposedly "dysfunctional" behaviors—are normal and necessary within the context of their experience. Our job as adults is not to break down their defenses, but to learn to listen to them and to see the very real strengths that are being used to operate those survival systems. Then it's a question of earning their trust, encouraging their strengths and modeling more productive ways of acting and communicating.

The Prevention First Experience

Bill: Of the things you've learned at PRC, was there one that you least expected to learn?

Pam: Definitely: the value of collaboration.   Its value to **me,** I mean.   I'd always believed in collaboration in the abstract—that it's important for people to work together, that none of us can do it alone, that everyone who's going to be affected by something needs to be in on its development—all that stuff.   But when it came to planning and structuring and writing a document, I really wanted complete control over the process.   Of course I never got it, because there is no such thing.   But I considered the need to collaborate and involve other people a threat to my freedom and my standards—and a very time-consuming process—and I secretly thought it would all be much better if I could just do it all by myself.

Then came the planning of the *Tools for Transformation* manual, on reclaiming cultural traditions in community-based prevention programs.   Alfred Jean-Baptiste, of the Participatory Research Group in Toronto, acted as consultant and collaborator on that one.   Alfred lives and breathes collaboration, and he was able to help me break into that mind-set better than anybody else could have done it.

I'll never forget the day I went to pick him up at the airport.   It was August, and I had about a month and a half to finish adapting the *Breaking the Chain* material into a manual, then synthesize a bunch of material from Alfred and seven other consultants and produce *Tools*—and get them both camera ready and printed by the end of September.   I was so scared I wouldn't get it all done that I felt paralyzed, and I couldn't get myself to write anything.   On the way back from the airport, Alfred gently suggested that perhaps my fear and my paralysis came from the fact that I thought I had to do everything all by myself. What a concept!

The next day we called up everybody we could think of who might want to have some input into the manual, and asked them all over for an impromptu planning session. Alfred facilitated and I took copious notes, and among us we hammered out an outline and structure. After the session was over Alfred fiddled with the outline, then I fiddled with it, then we gave it to Steven Guerra, PRC's director of program operations, so he could fiddle with it. Then Alfred went back to Canada and wrote a workshop model, and sent it on disk through the mail.

When it was time for me to start drafting the body of the manual, the words came out complete and unhindered—some of the best writing I'd ever done. Instead of constraining me, the collaborative nature of the planning process had freed me. I still don't quite understand it, but it was as if I'd become more than just one person. I hadn't sacrificed my standards: I'd transcended them.

Bill: Have you tried this process again to see if it was the process itself that produced that effect?

Yes, when we planned *Increase the Peace*, the manual on violence that came out this past Fall. We held several focus groups for that one, with participation by a number of former gang members. In those sessions we didn't pound out a complete outline, but we did delve deeply into the psychological roots of violence. And we had more sessions after I'd finished the outline and before I started writing. It was the same thing: I felt like I wasn't writing it by myself. I felt like a conduit for other people's experience, other people's emotional realities. My realities were there too, but they stayed in perspective because the other realities were so much larger. It felt really good to be "worked through" like that.

Bill: What's the most challenging project you've worked on in the prevention field?

Pam: They've all been challenging, if only because I have to keep learning so much. I guess the most challenging so far has been a collaborative project we worked on with the Rehabilitation Institute of Chicago (RIC), on substance abuse prevention for people with traumatic brain and spinal cord injuries. There was a lot of hard work and input by RIC staff and their advisory committee, but there was also a vast amount of information that I had to absorb and synthesize. It meant combining two fields, substance abuse prevention and rehabilitation from traumatic injury.

The manual that came out of that process was directed toward rehabilitation staff, and it synthesized information about prevention, rehabilitation, traumatic injury, intervention, treatment, family issues and ways of coping with the many life stresses that can follow injury. The manual ended up quite long. My part in the project lasted two years—and the project was going on before me and it's still going on now. They're training staff, starting special support groups and all sorts of wonderful things. They've also sold a lot of manuals!

Bill: Of all the projects you've worked on, is there one that you feel closest to, in terms of subject matter?

Pam: That would have to be the issue of *Common Ground* on Spirituality in Prevention. That subject is so abstract—actually, more nebulous than abstract—that I can get lost in it for hours and never get bored. I also believe the spiritual principles that are common to many cultures are essential to the real success of prevention programs. I think if we were to do that issue over we'd probably do it a little less from the head and a little more from the heart. But the reception for it has been wonderful. I think people in the field, and in the communities, are really hungry for materials and presentations on that subject.

Bill: What's it like working at Prevention First's Chicago office?

Pam: We have a lot of fun. We're all pretty driven, but we also like to laugh, so it balances itself out. The atmosphere is very interactive, very collaborative. Nobody has a little empire, with his own little projects. We all seem to get called in on everything, at different stages. I'm kind of a compulsive editor, so I get pulled into many projects near the end, when people have drafted things. I also like to spin concepts, so sometimes I'm in on conversations when people are planning things. And when I'm working on a document, I like to run ideas and drafts past people too. It makes for much better final products, and we all get to appreciate one another's skills much more when we see them at work. It also gets rid of that fear that comes from trying to do things in isolation.

Bill: Your new office set-up in Chicago seems particularly conducive to that kind of collaborative mix.

Pam: Yes. It's wonderful having the library in the center, and all the offices and meeting areas opening onto it. It makes it feel much more communal. And the best thing is that, almost as soon as we'd moved in, community-based prevention groups started using it as a training and meeting place, just like we hoped they'd do. We want the office to be a hub for collaborative prevention efforts in the Chicago area, and it's turning out that way. It feels very much alive.

Bill: A little while ago you talked about trying over and over again to find a way to make your "best" possible contribution to the world. Do you think you've found it?

Pam: I think it was there all along, but I was looking for it in jobs and titles and functions, so I never noticed it. I finally think I agree with those people who say that our best possible contribution is to be consistently friendly, respectful, loving people. I used to think that was too puny and insignificant, until I tried doing it for a day. Do you know how hard that is? I doubt I'll ever be able to do it consistently, but as long as I keep trying, everything else in my life seems to improve.

Personal Contributions and Challenges

Bill: What's your biggest challenge these days?

Pam: I guess it's juggling school and work and having a life. I'm almost through the master's program at DePaul's School for New Learning. The course content was fascinating, and each of us designed our own curriculum—with excellent guidance—but going back to school after all those years was a shock.

Bill: Was your decision to go back to school influenced by the kinds of writing you hope to do in the future?

Pam: Yes, and by the quality of writing and research I hope to do. I needed a more scholarly approach to my work, although I'd still rather keep the tone of the writing simple and casual. And I do have this fantasy about publishing lots of books.

Bill: Well, you're getting a start on that, since your master's project is a book.

Pam: Yes. I've just finished my Master Work, which is the School's equivalent of a thesis, outside of my work for Prevention First. It's a book called *Worth Protecting: Women, Men, and Freedom From Sexual Aggression*, with Terry Gorski as co-author. It should be coming out in March of 1995. Now we are working on a companion workbook, due out in the Fall of 1995.

Worth Protecting is a guide for women and men on preventing things like date rape and sexual manipulation. It takes a non-adversarial approach—compassionate toward both genders. I took many weeks' vacation time to do the drafts, and incorporated a lot of material from long meetings with Terry. Fortunately we agree on most aspects of the subject, but we still managed to have some lively debates. That book is truly a reflection of both people's ideas and knowledge. I think it had to be written by a woman and a man together.

I guess the biggest challenge in drafting *Worth Protecting* was in writing it so that it could be understood by people in the age groups at highest risk for date rape—ages 14 to 28. In order to do justice to the subject we had to include some concepts that high school-aged kids don't usually encounter, so we defined and described them in simple, concrete terms. That's not easy!

Bill: How has your experience in resuming your education influenced your thinking?

Pam: I'd been used to looking at the world in a limited number of ways, maybe adding one or two modes of thought each year. Then as soon as I started taking classes and working on all these projects I had all this information flying at me, and everything I read seemed to describe and interpret the world in a different way. So I've had to learn to remain open to them all, and fit them together, and discard what I can't use—but not too quickly, because I might be wrong. I find myself thinking about this stuff all the time. I've always been absent minded, but it's getting much worse. I've taken to sticking post-it notes onto my purse—or my person—just so I can remember who I'm supposed to call, or what errands I'm supposed to run on the way home.

Bill: Many people find that they can't work and go to school and have a life. They sort of suspend their lives until they get the degree.

Pam: I know. It's tempting, but I keep thinking how hypocritical that would be. Here I am writing about the importance of healthy, balanced lives. What would happen to the conviction behind that if I were to stop living and just study and work? We'll see, though. I'm sure I'm perfectly capable of hypocrisy.

I complain a lot, but I love it. And I keep thinking: five years ago—and for 10 years before that—I was stuck in jobs I didn't want, doing work that bored me and trying to find a chance to prove what I could do. Now I'm writing for a living, working for an organization I believe in—in a field I believe in—going for an advanced degree, and writing books. My confidence, which was so low for so long, is really starting to take off.

I guess if I can communicate anything as a writer, it's just like you said in your interview: There's hope. There's more hope than we can imagine.

Part II

The Writing Craft

Chapter 3

Inspiration and Direction

Beginning to Write

Pam: Are there any rules for aspiring writers?

Bill: Just one: Don't listen to people who dictate rules to aspiring writers. There's no secret. There is no single mechanism that unlocks the power to write. The key is not how one's writing is planned, or when and where you write, or what tools you use to capture the words. The mystery to be unlocked is in yourself and your relationship to the act of writing. If you want to create great writing, learn the fundamental mechanics of writing and then study yourself.

I think you also have to live before you can write. Every writer must create a deep well, filled not with ink but with experience. This well will be drawn from again and again for inspiration, motivation, places, characters, plots, stories, ideas, metaphors, and words.

Pam: Do you have any general advice for the aspiring writer in the substance abuse field?

Bill: I would tell the aspiring writer to read great writing, to experiment with different rituals of writing in order to understand his or her own writing psychology, and above all to write and write and write. Write every day. Has there ever been a book about writing that didn't include this admonition?

Where do you start? Start by collecting words—doodling with words. Collect ideas. Collect experiences. Collect observations of people and the world. Collect stories. Collect metaphors. These are the raw material of the writer. Start right now. Write in the margins or in a separate notebook your reactions to what you are reading on these pages. The moment the first words go onto paper, you are a writer.

You start by picking up the pen or turning the computer on and selecting the first word. Every work, including the best of our past and present literature, began with these small acts. My advice is: if you can't write full time, write part time; if you can't write for 10 hours a week, write for one hour a week; if you can't write a book, write an article; if you can't write an article, begin a journal. You simply must take action! If you want to write, you must find a way to write, no matter what constraints the universe has imposed on your life.

Pam: One thing I'd add to that is to look outside our own disciplines for clues. Some of the most important concepts I've come across have come from seemingly unrelated fields. I think our societal mania for specialization is slowing down our progress. Taking a step away from that mania sort of parallels the concept of holistic health. We're realizing we can't divide people into little pieces and expect our treatment of this or that piece to benefit the whole. Instead, we're beginning to take the whole person into account and think about how all the pieces work together.

I think it's that way with professional concepts and practices too. Even in my role for Prevention First, I can't just focus on information about addictions and public health promotion. If I do that I'll miss all the valuable information in the areas of philosophy, theology, history, management, psychology, mythology, anthropology, and all the rest. It all fits together, and the better my view of the whole, the better my perspective on my particular piece of that whole.

Journaling: Capturing Perceptions, Ideas and Feelings

Pam: How do you sustain a daily ritual of writing?

Bill: I think journaling is the foundation. Journaling is an exceptionally important technique to capture fleeting ideas and to work every day on the craft of writing. Journaling can be formal, like a daily diary entry, or very informal—I used to write on napkins and hotel receipts whenever worthy ideas chose to visit. Part of the trick of writing is capturing the best ideas and words before they flee back to their mysterious source. If not captured, they are usually gone forever. Always carrying pen and paper to take notes on one's own musings is exceptionally helpful to the new and experienced writer. I now carry spiral notebooks with me everywhere for just this purpose. Saving such scratched notes and organizing them by topic is the beginning of most of my papers and books. Notes incorporated into my book on the cultures of addiction and recovery spanned more than 15 years.

Writers need a place to store and incubate their ideas. They need little storage rooms within which to collect words, phrases, ideas, images, themes, titles, and stories. My journals are my storage rooms.

Pam: People seem to have a wide variety of places where they store those ideas.

Bill: The use of the notebook, the sketchbook, the journal, the diary, and the letter to stimulate creativity is referenced in the biographies of the world's most celebrated geniuses. It's worth pursuing these devices, if for no other reason than for the quality of the company.

Pam: What kinds of things can be captured in the journaling process?

Bill: Journaling can take many forms. The experiential diary is a tool to heighten emotional receptiveness and to master writing that is affective in tone and content. The event diary sharpens one's reporting skills. The intellectual diary is a way to catch fleeting ideas and pin them on paper. A writing diary is an interesting variation on journaling. I recently read the diary that John Steinbeck kept while writing *The Grapes of Wrath*. I was fascinated to see how he used the recording of his daily writing activities to increase and sustain his writing productivity.

The journal is to the writer what rehearsal is to the actor. Journal entries can later be mined for ideas, words, and images that can be appropriated into one's public works. There are all sorts of journals. They are so deliciously private, there aren't any rules for them. What they all share in common is the regular ritual of writing. If you aspire to write, you must write—that is the most fundamental principle. Journaling is an excellent way to prime the writing pump and keep it primed.

Pam: I've heard you mention that women throughout history have found the journal a particularly important tool. Why is that?

Bill: I see this in terms of the personal and institutionalized violence against women. In this context, the diary or journal became the safest of relationships. It was the one vehicle through which women could express their secret selves without fear of retribution. The movement out of silence, the discovery of voice, began for many women on the pages of a diary or journal. In a world in which women only had value in relationship to another—usually a man or a child—the diary became the one place to experience self outside of relationship.

Anaïs Nin is unquestionably the most famous of women diarists. When she died in 1977, she had produced more than 35,000 handwritten pages covering her experiences from age 11 to 71. Ten volumes of her diary have been published. Nin describes her writing through the metaphor of breathing. It's a beautiful metaphor. Experiencing herself suffocating in a world of constraint, she said writing became the breath of life.

Pam: And her life became relatively free of constraint, if I recall correctly. So maybe the diary was also a place where she could transform the self into someone who was able to take chances and break free.

Writing as Self-Exploration and Therapy

Pam: Have you ever consciously used writing as an emotional safety valve?

Bill: I'm not sure to what extent I unconsciously use writing as a safety valve. I've always been able to express thoughts and feelings on paper that were difficult for me to express out loud. There have been times of personal and professional crisis when I've consciously used writing as a tool for catharsis and self-examination. This writing, however, is not material that I ever seek to publish. Writing that has served as great personal therapy rarely possesses artistic value.

Pam: Or professional value. What would be an example of a time when you used writing as a pure form of release?

Bill: Early in my career, I mentored a number of people who worked as one-person drug programs across Illinois. In a week of professional horror, I was called to intervene with one of these individuals who had relapsed and become sexually involved with an adolescent client. After driving this person to Chicago for entry into treatment, debriefing his agency peers and assisting in meetings with his clients to process his fall from grace, I returned to Bloomington in a state of exhaustion, pain and confusion. Before debriefing these events in supervision, I spent three hours writing to purge myself of my own sense of personal and professional betrayal and to meditate on my own personal vulnerability and my need for structure and support. This writing helped extract meaning from a very difficult experience.

Pam: And I bet the insights that came out of that experience—and the journaling that followed it—added fuel to many of the professional works you'd write later. Maybe the journaling itself wasn't fit for professional consumption, but it was an essential step in an important process. I'm very much interested in the relationship between "therapeutic" introspection and good writing, for two reasons. One is that there's a tendency to be professionally suspicious of a work if its development process could be considered "therapeutic" for the author. The other is that it's so tempting for newer writers to see their introspective ramblings as art, or as a potential source of healing for others. It's difficult to find the balance between the need to experience and the need to detach.

Bill: Have you considered some of your professional creative processes therapeutic for you?

Pam: I'm always leery of the word "therapeutic." I think that much of what we label therapeutic is really just healthy growth and development. Anything I do—even standing in line at the supermarket—can qualify as therapeutic if it in some way increases my understanding, empathy, and sense of perspective. I think most of the things I've written have been therapeutic in that sense. If the process of writing something isn't therapeutic, then I didn't do it right. But I think if it's **only** therapeutic, then it's just journaling.

Bill: To what extent does your writing come out of personal experience and insight?

Pam: When I think about it, almost everything I've written that I've really liked—and felt some momentum at work in writing it—was first inspired by some specific insight that was important in my own life. I can usually remember the day it hit me, the circumstances, the emotions, everything. Generally the insight was preceded by a painful time—some kind of stress or confusion, a problem I couldn't solve with information, logic, and will. The circumstances under which the insight came might be quite different from those I'm writing about now, but the insight cuts through those differences.

Bill: Do you find that journaling can bring you closer to that moment of insight?

Pam: I find that journaling can be a good tool for catching the insight when it occurs, but the insight usually doesn't occur until after I've stopped throwing words at the problem, and just stayed for a while in that place where I'm not sure of anything any more. I used to be terrified of that place, because I only got there by being in pain, and finally had to admit that I couldn't control the process or the outcome. That's hard stuff for most of us! The temptation to distract oneself from uncomfortable feelings is enormous.

Bill: You said you "used to be terrified of that place." Does that mean you no longer fear this place of uncertainty?

Pam: No, I'm sure I still fear it. But I'm also kind of curious—and even glad—once I realize that's where I am. I've come to associate it more with relief than with pain. I've come to recognize that gut feeling that says "something is happening that I don't understand. My opinions aren't going to get me out of it, either, but when it's over I'll be better off than I've ever been." I've heard people talk about "walking through the discomfort." That means not intellectualizing it, not escaping it, but respecting it, and knowing that that's where the insight is.

It's like those wonderful images Joseph Campbell talked about, those vast, dark caves with ancient paintings scratched on the wall. If I follow my fear and back out of the cave, I'll never learn what I went in there to learn. There's a wonderful story, and I wish I could remember where I'd heard it. The student asks, "How long must I remain in the dark?" and the teacher replies, "Until you learn to see in the dark." Of course, talking to the right people can also help the process go more quickly and smoothly.

Bill: How do you use these insights in your writing? Is there any danger that you'll be pursuing some personal agenda that won't be relevant to others?

Pam: Of course. That's one of the greatest dangers for all writers, whether we're working from insight or from pure intellect. I think after the insight comes we have to get very detached and scientific about it. How universal is this? Is it something that's important to everyone, or just to people in certain circumstances, or just to me? Whenever I have an important insight—as soon as it's cooled off enough that I can see what it is—I start talking to people about it. And if a number of people light up and say "Yes! It's that way for me, too, but I never thought about it in those terms!" then I know I have something. And I start whittling away the pieces that are just me and my own stuff, and see what's left.

Bill: When do you start writing about it?

Pam: All along the way, in different forms. As you were saying earlier about journaling, it's very helpful just to write about something, even in its unformed state. It becomes clearer. Eventually my intentions become clear enough that I know what kind of piece I'd like to write, for what audience, what purpose, whatever. Then it's time to start reading and asking around, to find out if it's needed, and if it's already been written. If it has been written, then I don't get to write it—but at least I get to read it. That helps me integrate the insight into my experience and get some perspective on it. Then I can start to build on it and move onto something new.

Bill: I think that process is important, discovering what within your experience is so universal as to find resonance in the lives of your readers. I could use as an example what we are doing right now. My personal experiences with the process of writing are only important to the extent that they help other writers better understand and enhance their own creative processes. It's not what is unique about my writing process that is important; it's that which can be used to stimulate the writing processes of others.

Thinking Mentors and Writing Mentors

Pam: What do you think the beginning writer needs most?

Bill: Beginning writers need someone to affirm that the effort is worthwhile, that the process of placing words on paper has meaning and value. They need to find people who will fire their imagination and recognize their personal power. Above all, they must avoid people who will do harm to the emerging writing self. The beginning writer needs to be heard and encouraged.

Pam: Hear, hear. But it's difficult to be a good mentor, and it's difficult to find one. It's hard to believe in a writer who has all these rough edges, and it's hard to find people who are capable of taking that "leap of faith." One has to weed out a lot of well-meaning people who are stuck in their doubts and their own opinions—even if they often sound like they know what they're talking about.

On the other hand, I think it's equally important to have somebody who's willing to tell you if they think you're off base—and to have enough mentors going that you can check it out with others in case that person was off base. Sometimes those can be the most valuable lessons a mentor can teach: that it's possible to survive being wrong, it's possible for the wisest mentor to be wrong, and it's possible to forgive our heroes for being fallible.

Bill: I know it can be hard to find mentors when you're new to a particular field. The same lack of belief in one's potential that needs the mentor can make it harder to find the mentor. How have you handled that challenge?

Pam: My first hurdle was to get over the feeling that the relationship wouldn't be worth a potential mentor's time and energy. I needed to learn one thing: No matter what my level of skill or talent might be, if it's a good match, the mentoring relationship would help the mentor as much as it helped me. Human beings have a basic need to pass on to others what we've learned. I've found the concept of "generativity" useful in understanding that need. At its most basic, generativity is the desire of one generation to pass something on to the next. The only time that need doesn't show up is if we're caught up in professional jealousy and feel like there's only so much talent to go around so we'd better keep it all for ourselves. Otherwise, though, we understand that the best way to learn something is to teach it, and the best way to get what we need is to give it to others.

The next step for me was to practice recruiting mentors in other areas of life. Almost anything—a hobby, participation in a group, or whatever—can serve as a practice ground. Most people have been recruiting mentors all their lives, but never thought about it in those terms. It's a lot less intimidating to practice in areas of life that we don't identify with so intensely. Then when we've seen how well we can handle the mentoring relationship, and how much benefit it brings to the mentor, it's easier to do it in our field of choice.

I think it's also important to learn to identify the types of personalities and characteristics that are compatible with ours, and gravitate toward those people. For example, somebody might be the best writer in the world, or the best theoretician in the world, but if he or she intimidates me on a personal level, that's not going to be my best match for a mentor. I don't function well when I'm intimidated, although some people do. It's a question of what does and doesn't work for us as individuals.

I found Rilke's book, *Letters to a Young Poet* very useful in my efforts to learn about mentoring relationships and to get the courage to seek them out. *Letters* is a beautiful and moving look into a very respectful mentor/mentee relationship. It's Rilke's letters to a young man who wrote to him and sent some copies of his poetry. The letters show a wonderful balance of honesty, respect and affection.

How important have personal mentors been to your writing?

Bill: I think the most important mentors I had were people early in my career who told me that I should be writing, that what I was thinking was important enough to share with the world. People like Dr. Doug Bey, an early supervising psychiatrist, and Dr. Alan Walker, a distinguished professor from Goddard College, spoke of my duty to write and publish ideas I was sharing with them. They didn't just suggest it—they demanded it. It wasn't that I was important, it was that what I was saying was important. They framed it as a professional obligation that one could not ignore in good conscience. Their affirmation of my ideas and personal challenges to me were very important to the beginnings of my professional writing. Other mentors were important primarily by influencing how I think.

Pam: Who would be an example of that kind of mentor?

Bill: Bill Coats. I worked with Bill at the Dangerous Drugs Commission. He influenced me and my subsequent writing in two very important ways.

First, his values were very up-front in how he defined and approached solving problems. He really cared about the problems and issues we were addressing and used a very clear set of values that shaped his decisions and actions. He taught me to explicitly define the values that are often hidden in our responses to human problems.

Second, he taught me how to think in pictures. I saw problems in words, outlines and chains of logic. Bill saw them in pictures. He worked to enhance my visual thinking—my ability to "see" a problem, to diagram it in its relationship to other things. He taught me a lot about wrestling with complexity that has deeply influenced my writing.

Pam: Who else besides your mentors has contributed to your writing?

Bill: I think there's another kind of person who is essential to the writer, who could not properly be called a mentor. This is the person who is a sounding board, who provides a kind of laboratory culture within which one's best thinking can grow. It seems most creative geniuses had this sort of accomplice that were essential to their creative processes. A Sherlock Holmes without a Dr. Watson would be unthinkable. I think young and old writers need this kind of catalyst to their creativity.

Pam: Yes. And I find it particularly valuable to do this with people who think differently than I do. I like to use "nuts-and-bolts" people in that role. These people often point out the obvious—like where it is I'm losing people. They can serve as a sort of grounding.

Mentoring Yourself

Pam: So how does the new writer sustain his or her work when mentors and other supportive people just can't be found?

Bill: If you can't find mentors—and there will be such periods—you have to learn to mentor yourself. You have to develop the art of self-dialogue and internalize the mentoring functions of coaxing, coaching, cheering and correcting. There are periods in one's life that demand such self-containment, self-possession and self-nurturing.

I think you can also find mentors between the covers of books. Writing creates a product that has the unique quality of enduring accessibility. There are people of influence and support in my life that I may not always be able to reach, but I can always reach my bookshelves. And I really mean a direct comparison here. I can experience a sense of relationship and personal encouragement from some authors through exposure to their written words. There are people who have meant a great deal to me simply because they existed and created a body of radiant writing. I can get re-centered or push myself in certain directions based on the literature I feed myself. Carefully choosing and experiencing literature are vehicles of self-creation and self-renewal.

Pam: What writers in the field should aspiring writers be reading?

Bill: Aspiring writers should be reading a wide spectrum of great writers both within and outside the field. Reading within the field has two distinct purposes: first, to master the basic history and knowledge base of the field, and second, to master the language in which the field communicates.

There are several authors within the field I would recommend. If you want to know how to write history, read David Musto's, *The American Disease* or Ernie Kurtz's, *Not God: A History of Alcoholics Anonymous*. If you want examples of how technical research can be translated into language accessible to service practitioners, read Sidney Cohen's *The Chemical Brain* or Ron Siegal's *Intoxication*. If you want to read a combination of directness and gentleness in confronting the field, read Charlotte Kasl's, *Many Roads, One Journey*. If you want to read a book that inspires, read Cecil William's, *No Hiding Place*. If you want to read clarity and comprehensiveness in an academic text, read Jerome

Levin's, *Alcoholism: A Biopsychosocial Approach.* I think all of these are examples of skilled writers doing service to the field.

Writing Workshops

Pam: How about writing workshops? Have you found these helpful?

Bill: I've never been to one. I think aspiring writers need contact with other writers for support and feedback. Although I lacked access to formal writing workshops, I had relationships with other writers that were very important to me during my early career. I know many people for whom such workshops helped refine their craft, and in a few cases, led to their discovery and the eventual publication of their work. Writers who have worked within the best of the master-apprentice tradition are very fortunate. Attending writing workshops is one way to cultivate such relationships.

Pam: Writing workshops also have the virtue of forcing you to write. But it can be hard to bring our early efforts into situations where a whole bunch of people can see what's wrong with them. I think there are some awkward stages when we're not sure what we want to say or what we want to do with it. How do new writers get through these stages, and "walk through" the embarrassment of being imperfect?

Bill: I think writers have to flounder for a while until they develop a knowledge of their talents and a clear vision of how they want to relate to and change the world. Each of us has to write his or her way through immaturity and confusion. A reasonable goal for the developing writer is to write today with more clarity and power than you did yesterday.

If we wait to write until we get our act together, the writing somehow never gets done. Writing isn't about waiting; it's about writing. It may be that the writing is part of how we get our act together. It's a funny thing about the arts. In pursuing the creative process, in seeking to refine our abilities and in offering up the product of our skills to others, we end up healing and nurturing ourselves. And in healing ourselves, we open up more significant opportunities to heal the world.

Pam: But that's the whole concept of reciprocity: Whatever we give, we get—whether that's effort, or healing, or less pleasant things. I think that cuts through all disciplines, and all areas of life. It may be a more fundamental law of nature than gravity.

Writing Projects

Pam: For a long time I've had a tendency to work on one project at a time, and harness my obsessive/compulsive nature in honing in on that project. But I'm beginning to see some disadvantages to that—like getting stuck and immobile when I hit an impasse, or hitting a dry period when the project's over.

Do you work on more than one writing project at a time?

Bill: I always have multiple projects going on at the same time. Some projects need to be completed in short bursts of writing activity separated by time and reflection, while others need sustained, focused activity from beginning to end. When I'm not working on deadlines, I simply look over my various works in progress and see which one elicits my excitement. Three hours later I may tire of this subject and shift to another project that is underway. The variety helps prevent writing fatigue and allows me to achieve a higher level of writing productivity.

Pam: You've been involved in writing books, monographs, articles, planning documents, and research reports. What are some of the differences among those types of works?

Bill: I think there are only two kinds of writing. There's production writing: a form of technical writing that is rather mechanical in nature. The product has a feel of roteness and anonymity. I consider much of the grant writing, report writing, and research writing to be this kind of production writing. Production writing is a chore—you crank it out as efficiently and quickly as possible. Process writing, in contrast, engages the soul of the writer in a way that the product as it emerges could only come from this person. It contains a high level of originality and is presented in a uniquely personal style.

Pam: Which is most difficult for you?

Bill: Writing research reports is really difficult because it requires avoidance of my natural style. Production writing requires squeezing all of the emotion out of my words and squeezing me out of my treatment of the subject. Unless the implications of the research findings are profound, I find this kind of writing to be very lifeless and boring.

I'm excited about a new approach to research that we have been involved with at the Institute. This approach supplements traditional quantitative research with a kind of qualitative data the folks at Highlander Center in Tennessee call "people's knowledge." The research involves a structured approach to listening to people's own perceptions about their needs, problems and potential solutions. This approach to research is very empowering. It provides a vehicle through which the consumers of our services can tell in their own voice what has and has not been helpful in our interventions into their lives.

Pam: I can see that approach in your work. The personal lives of clients really come through. They're not washed away in the usual sea of statistical analysis.

Bill: There are stories researchers can't tell, stories so powerful that the words of those who live the stories must be allowed to stand on their own, unedited and uninterpreted. I'm regularly humbled in my efforts to summarize the findings that emerge from our client interviews, whether they be cocaine-addicted women or adolescents living on the streets. I am awe-struck by their unfathomable capacity for suffering. I am speechless in the face of their sheer endurance and resilience. I am often left questioning the source of their continued will to struggle and resist. When I try to portray their lives in my writing, I must quote them because I have no words that can do justice to their stories.

Having Something to Say

Pam: What do you consider the most important element of writing?

Bill: Having something to say. Even extraordinary skills in the writing craft are meaningless if you have nothing to say. Technical skill cannot compensate for a lack of heart and vision. Writing craft cannot mask empty words. Our writing is ultimately only as good as the clarity, originality and value of what we see, think and feel. Writers are people who have something to say. Where there's a message, there's a writer waiting to be born.

Pam: When it comes to producing ideas, one concept that's helped me a lot is one that I ran into in a little book on time management, many years ago. I don't even remember the name of the author or the title of the book. The author said that inspiration—a new idea—is really nothing more than the combination of elements that one hadn't thought of combining before. And when I think about most of the "new" ideas I've had or heard of others having, they're really new combinations. Even the incredible things that Mozart wrote were just new combinations of the same old notes!

Bill: What would be some examples of that within our field?

Pam: Look at some of the wonderful things that are happening in the prevention field. People are combining basic prevention with things like holistic health, community development, spirituality, cultural traditions, leadership development, psychology, addiction and recovery principles—these are all important facets of human and community life, so they belong in prevention, and they take it to a higher and deeper place.

I think everything in life really does fit together on some level—it's just a question of how. We're so used to thinking of the elements of life as separate pieces in a machine, and through the centuries we've taken it all apart, as if that would help us understand it better. I think in some ways it does, but in some ways it limits our understanding. Now it's time to start putting it all back together. It's a question of courage—of having the courage to try different combinations of ideas, knowing that we're going to be wrong some of the time.

Beginning a Book

Pam: What part of the book-writing process do you find most difficult?

Bill: The greatest challenge and pleasure for me is in the mastery of the ideas and conveying the basic message within a book. The most difficult writing for me is always at the beginning. I do more rewriting of the early pages of a project than in all the remaining pages. I have to write my way into the project and then come back and make sure this awkward beginning can be made consistent with the tone and style achieved within the rest of the work.

Pam: How would you describe the experience of starting a book?

Bill: I think every author has the desire to write one book that is the crowning signature of his or her life. When I begin a book, I wonder early on if this book will be my signature.

I look on each book as an adventure and feel a special exhilaration and sense of wonder about where this particular book will take me. There really is a sense of the unknown. Each one of my books has evolved in a direction I could never have foreseen when the first words were written.   It's the unpredictable course of this adventure that I still enjoy.

There's also a special sense of power with each beginning—a screaming leap into the unknown. You may have a thousand fears and insecurities, but at the moment you sit down to begin a creative project, you must write with the power and authority of God. When you stand up, you re-embrace your humanity with all your petty foibles, but in the writing hour, you must write as if you controlled the universe.

Pam: Yikes! The universe would be in terrible trouble if I controlled it! I'm very absent-minded. Let me think for a second and see if I recognize any of those feelings from the process of working on *Worth Protecting*. I think I was conscious of having to take one stance that I considered egotistical: the assumption that I could write a book in the first place, even—or especially—with a co-author of Terry's stature. The first chapter was very difficult to draft, and I ended up rewriting it three times—completely—before it clicked. And the one that finally clicked came out almost effortlessly, seven months later.

By the second chapter, though, I started coming up with some unexpected ideas about how to present the material that Terry and I had talked about so many times, and I'd written so many outlines about. Just knowing that new ideas were still coming out put me in a sort of "flow" state, where I was working less from conscious control than from an intuitive sense. It felt as if all I had to do was get quiet enough, and I'd be able to hear it. Like the idea that a reflection is least distorted in water that's completely still. I drafted several chapters in that state—definitely not feeling as if I was controlling the universe, but trusting that the words that were going through me were in harmony with the universe. So it was sort of the opposite of your concept, but it served the same purpose.

Bill: Actually your concept is very close to mine. I'm not talking about ego here. I'm talking about using the self as an instrument. The boldness I describe is not an assertion of ego but a refusal to let one's petty ego stand in the way of the words that need to be written. It's embracing the flow of the words rather than fearing that they won't come or fighting them.

Chapter 4

Topic Development and Research

Selecting the Topic

Pam: In terms of choosing and exploring topics and themes, where do you think the new writer should start?

Bill: There are two areas in which writers can make significant contributions. The first is to describe the center of our experience that is invisible because of its closeness and commonness. The gifted writer can describe such a phenomenon and have readers say, "I knew that," and yet have them know that in a more important way because of the writer's ability to isolate and depict it. The writer who helps us more consciously know what we already know has made a great contribution.

This ability to capture the common is particularly important during times of change. The task of the writer in such times is to find that center of quietness within the eye of the hurricane and describe the turmoil that surrounds. Naming and describing can enhance our sense of personal control over change.

Pam: It can also bring dignity. I don't know why, but dignity seems to be connected with stillness. What is the second area in which the writer can contribute.

Bill: The second area is by moving into, or beyond, the far frontiers of our experience. I think it was Paul Tillich who once said that the boundary was the best place for acquiring knowledge. From the boundary, the writer can look back and describe our familiar territory in new ways. Based on their new knowledge, they can force us to redefine ourselves and our perception of the world. This is the writer as explorer and risk-taker. This is the part of the writing process that can be intoxicating. I'm exhilarated by the movement from the familiar into the unknown. I can feel my heart pounding when, with full consciousness, I move past that boundary into the unknown frontier. The fear and anticipation are exhilarating.

Pam: Probably the most common piece of advice writers hear is "write about what you know." Any reactions to this advice?

Bill: I would admonish beginning writers: write not just about what you know but also about what you wish to know. Let your excitement at new discoveries energize your research and writing.

Each writer must write about that which excites his or her imagination. Regardless of the nature of the emotion, there must be passion and intensity with which the writer approaches the topic. The answer to the question, "What should I write about?" is best reframed as the question, "What do I feel intensely about?" We write best about that which arouses our passions.

Pam: How do you select the topics you write about?

Bill: Much of the activity of my life is guided by the answers to two questions. From the life of Bucky Fuller, I've learned to regularly look at my field of endeavor and ask: "What needs to be done?" From the life of Joseph Campbell, I've learned to periodically look within myself and ask: "Where is your bliss—that focus of study and activity that elicits passion and commitment?" I concentrate my writing and training activities where the answers to those two questions intersect.

Pam: Yes! But how does one find one's bliss under all this debris? I think for most people our hearts—or our souls, or whatever you want to call them—do give out clear messages. Somewhere we know what we really believe, what we really feel, what's important to us—and maybe even what the truth is. But those messages can get drowned out by things like fear, other people's expectations of us, or old images that don't work any more.

Ironically, I find that one of the best ways of finding out if an idea is truly important to me is to tell other people about it. If the idea really reaches deep inside me—and if I'm ready to articulate it—other people are more likely to feel the enthusiasm and react with enthusiasm. How much do other people contribute to your choice of topics?

Bill: Many of my topics come from listening to the needs of the field. It's like I'm the student, and the field is my teacher. The field gives me my writing assignments. I submit them in the form of articles, monographs, books, speeches, and workshops. The constituents of the field grade them based on whether my words touch and inform their experience.

Pam: So you listen and respond?

Bill: Yes, in two very different ways. At one level, I select topics by responding to direct requests from the field—from a collective call to write a paper or book exploring a particular area. But there is another level. This is responding to the needs of the field that the field has yet to even recognize or articulate. They need it but they don't know they need it until I give them my offering. The writer achieves this through an empathic identification with the field in a manner not unlike the empathic identification between a counselor and his or her client. This is not paternalistic arrogance—a belief that I, and only I, know what is best for the field. It's vigilance in listening and observing. Part of one's service to a professional field is listening to its unspoken, as well as spoken, needs.

There are, finally, some topics that seem to select me. There are some ideas that just won't go away; they just keep coming back to pester me. I discharge some ideas into my writing so they will stop haunting me.

Pam: How does this process differ from the process you use to pick training topics?

Bill: As a trainer, most of your topics are dictated by other people. Someone calls up and asks you to do a workshop on cocaine-exposed infants. While some of my writing is dictated in a similar manner, particularly writing related to the Institute's research activities, I find with the books and monographs that I have more freedom of personal selection.

Pam: Do you express your ideas differently in writing than you do in training?

Bill: I've always felt that ideas expressed in writing constitute a greater commitment than ideas expressed in speech.   I may discuss particular ideas as a forum for exploration, but the written presentation of those ideas constitutes a far bolder act of advocacy.   One is much more likely to be called upon to defend what one has written than what one has espoused in casual discourse.   The shift from oral to written communication calls for a more critical pruning of one's ideas and words.

Pam: Yes.   You leave a trail.   What do you see as the limits of the range of topics a writer can address?

Bill: Each writer must discover his or her own limits.   These limits should come from within rather than through some external source's definition of what we can or can't do.   Pushing the boundaries of those limits is often where great discoveries lie.

Pam: I know some people believe a writer has to be able to answer any question that he or she poses.   What do you think?

Bill: We don't have to have all the answers, but I think writers must be very passionate about the importance of the questions.   I think Anaïs Nin was right when she characterized the disease of our age as a loss of faith and hope.   In a world of darkness, the writer must determine whether the mission is to document the darkness or create light.   That choice separates the reporters from the healers and visionaries.   Writers don't need to have all the answers but I believe they have an obligation to bring a healing message—a message of hope.

Pam: What is that message?

Bill: I think one message is that our problems and crises afford opportunities for transformation, opportunities to move forward toward more meaningful levels of experience and achievement.   The message we preach to addicted clients must be a message we ourselves hear and heed.   The same deep inner shifts our clients make into health we can make into the future of our own field.   If we say that a new self can be created within the cocoon of the old, then we have to be open to the possibility that a new and dynamic organization can arise from within the shell of a decaying one.   Writers can help infuse an openness to participate in these evolutionary and transformative processes.

Pam: And in many cases we have to continue to be open to personal transformation ourselves in order to catalyze—or even participate in—the transformation of our organizations. I don't know anyone who can't stand to grow some more.

Bill: Life isn't going to rearrange itself for anyone; it moves forward with all its beauty and ugliness in unrelenting progression. Our only choice is to find the sweetness of daily life even when such sweetness is hidden in the midst of injustice, cruelty, stupidity and vulgarity. Each of us can be the antidote to the poison we find around us. Writers can provide part of the antidote to poisons that harm us individually and collectively. I really believe that when we experience and share joy, we decrease the infectiousness of pain and hatred.

As a writer, I always face the question of whether I just tell the story or whether I offer some hope of healing or reconciliation. Do we tell the tale of horror or the tale of heroism or both? They almost always co-exist if we explore a story with sufficient depth and breadth.

Pam: Yes, and if we leave out the hope, I believe we really do fight against it. I came to the realization some years ago that there's more than enough evidence in the world for despair, and there's more than enough evidence for hope. It becomes our decision—sometimes purely our decision—which body of evidence we concentrate on. And I do know one thing for sure: In ways that I understand, and in ways that I don't understand, my level of success or failure will be affected by my expectation of success or failure. Even people who claim to have no faith are usually willing to acknowledge that, because they've experienced it. We've all experienced it, over and over again.

Bill: That could apply on a personal level too.

Pam: Exactly! This principle seems to be reflected everywhere. If I'm driving down a country road and I see a horse running through the field to my left, and I watch that horse run as I drive, pretty soon my car will start to drift to the left, even though I'm not conscious of steering in that direction. Our lives and efforts do the same thing. If we focus on positive prospects, our lives grow more positive. Sometimes we just work better and make better decisions when we believe in ourselves and our chances. Sometimes we just don't get in our own way as much because we're not so anxious. Sometimes other people feel our confidence and cooperate more.

And sometimes it just doesn't make sense, but events seem to make way for us. These things don't always happen in ways that seem positive or helpful at the time. They might seem like obstacles and frustrations, but at some point along the line we turn back and see a clear thread leading from obstacle to obstacle, turning point to turning point, taking us exactly where we needed to go. If we didn't have some kind of vision, some kind of faith, could we have kept going? Would we have bothered?

And, of course, I choose to believe that there's hope. If I don't—and if I don't convey that in the things I write—how can I ever convince anyone else that there's hope?

Respecting the Topic

Pam: How would you suggest that writers approach topics that are beyond their own experience?

Bill: They must bring the topics within their experience.

Pam: How do you do this?

Bill: Writers have to first bring the topic within the range of their own senses—they must experience the issue. I can give you a recent example of this. You asked me some time ago to participate in a discussion forum and write a follow-up paper on the role of spirituality in substance abuse prevention. I approached this broad topic by preparing a detailed outline as if I were writing a book on the subject. The chapters on the outline gave me a variety of potential areas of focus for my paper. The discussion forum touched on a number of areas in my outline but focused particularly on creating a definition of spirituality that could provide an integrating motif for our discussions. I chose to write my paper on the working definition which had been created within this meeting. Whereas, many other areas of the topic I would have approached with aloofness, my chosen topic could be easily accessed through the intensity of my experience within the meeting.

Pam: This sometimes comes up for me when I'm given an assignment to write about people in circumstances I've never experienced. I've found that, in order to write effectively, I first have to find those core things that we have in common. Those core commonalities may be based on outer experiences that are quite different, but if they're genuine, they give the work the depth and energy that it would otherwise lack.

Bill: How does this fit in with your experience of insight?

Pam: It fits in amazingly well. I don't know if it's chance, or my subconscious, or divine intervention, but even when I'm working on something that's beyond my experience, the insights that are going to add depth to my writing seem to come along at the right time. And, of course, there are always a few in there on ice, waiting for the appropriate occasion.

Bill: It sounds like you put some effort into becoming intimate with the topic. I believe a writer must do that—experience the topic from inside rather than as an intellectual tourist. One must also conduct this exploration with humility and respect—you must respect your topic.

Pam: How does the writer demonstrate or violate this respect?

Bill: There is a kind of literary subjugation through which the writer's subject is stolen rather than honored and elucidated. When a journalist writes an article about teen violence that only gives lurid details of blood and mayhem, this is cheap voyeurism. The actors in this real story are being exploited for the reader's emotional titillation and the writer's profit. If you're going to bring me the story of a 16-year-old killer, you've got to help me understand the external and internal forces that helped pull the trigger. You've got to make the victims and the offenders come to life for me. The topic and the characters must be respected.

Nowhere is such disrespect more evident than in this culture's response to cocaine-abusing women and their children. If you're going to tell me the story of this mother, how can you deny me the story of her grandmother who has assumed her caretaking role? If you're going to tell me about the deficits of her child, you have to tell me about the growing evidence of this child's capacity to physically and spiritually overcome these limitations. Telling the truth is telling the whole story. If we tell the story of a community's frailty, we must also speak of its strength. Telling only part of the truth is a lie of omission that always has the potential for harm.

Pam: In the example of drug-exposed babies, how much harm resulted when the whole story wasn't told?

Bill: We portrayed them as all Black at a time when cocaine use was overwhelmingly White—shaming, demoralizing and further disempowering African-American communities. We exaggerated the risks and consequences of fetal cocaine exposure, some for ideological and personal advantage. We did enormous violence to these children through our labeling and predictions of their inevitable and sustained failure. There are untold numbers of infants who will suffer more developmental harm from being labeled a "crack baby" than from the effects of prenatal cocaine exposure. We spoke of the negative influences in their environments and were silent about the resources in these same environments. We spoke of their risks and ignored their resiliency. Our stories were politically exploited to create new laws to punish addicted women and, in the name of protecting children, drove these women out of the primary health care system, dramatically increasing the risks to their unborn children. Even where treatment resources were added as a result of this story, women were demeaned by a policy that implied they had value only because of their role as breeders and caretakers of this culture's children. Yes, I think our failure to tell this whole story—and the sensationalist approach to this story—did considerable damage.

Pam: How much of that damage came out of our desire to tackle a "hot topic" when we didn't have enough information? And how do you deal with the temptation to jump on one of those bandwagons?

Bill: There is often the writer's impulse to catch the crest of a hot topic within the field. I've tried to resist that pull and carefully select subject material that won't become stale. When considering a lengthy work, I often ask myself: "Will this topic and my treatment of it still be relevant and appropriate for the field in ten or twenty years?" I write many articles that try to put so-called "hot topics" in perspective or seek to deal with an immediate crisis within the field, but in my more substantive works I try to generate material that will age well and provide a lasting contribution. I'm usually more interested in the permanence of an issue than its immediacy.

Pam: It also occurs to me that, no matter how much writers can do to try to right a problem like the coverage of cocaine-exposed babies, we can never do it justice. I mean, the harm is done. If we really believe in prevention, we'll prevent the iatrogenic (intervention-caused harm) effects of our own words. We'll make sure we don't cause more problems than we've set out to solve.

It also makes me wonder what we're writing about these days that we might be doing in an unbalanced or potentially misleading way. In the prevention field, I think referring to people and communities as "at risk" has a strong potential for counterproductive—and actually destructive—effects. Labels are very powerful medicine. They can clarify the problem and initiate the healing process, or they can blow the problem up out of proportion, until it takes all attention and energy away from the solution.

Do you see any parallel to this in the treatment field?

Bill: The treatment side of the field has a long history of such labeling. One of the more recent episodes is the mislabeling of large numbers of adolescents. Thousands of adolescents were diagnosed with primary addictive diseases with no body of clinical evidence to justify such a diagnosis. I think the issue of labeling is an important issue to be addressed during this decade.

Pam: I wonder how many more of these issues we're missing.

On another subject: Once you've identified a topic clearly, how do you decide how to treat it?

Bill: The treatment of the subject is primarily determined by the purpose for which I'm writing. With each article, I ask myself: "What do I want this product to achieve?" There are primary and secondary purposes that must be sorted out. One project questions, another informs, another confronts, another persuades, another entertains, and still another inspires. I try to design each article or book to best achieve the experience I'm trying to provide for the reader. To structure a piece of writing in this way is to sculpt that one vessel that is meant to hold the story you are trying to tell. How I want my written words to affect the reader determines my approach to the subject.

Pam: How do you communicate this purpose to the reader?

Bill: With the kind of writing I do, my purpose is usually explicitly communicated to the reader in the opening sentences. Most of my articles open with a single thesis statement and everything else in the article is chosen to support or illustrate this statement. I try to tell the reader the destination of our journey and the route we will take to get there, and I also try to regularly post "you are here" signs along the way. This is a way of keeping the reader from getting lost in my words or stories.

Author and Audience

Pam: To what extent do you write for yourself?

Bill: I try to write the kind of books I like to read. When I get tired of waiting for someone else to write the book I need, I write it myself. As I'm composing, I am at that moment both author and audience.

With *Critical Incidents*, I wrote the book I needed early in my career but couldn't find. By serendipity of my agency settings, I had more support than most of my early peers within the field, but needed oh-so-much more than I had. Writing that book was like passing along a map, marking all the hidden hazards to a younger generation of workers. I wanted to chart out the ethical land mines within our field so newcomers would at least recognize when they were in dangerous territory.

Pam: I've heard that many writers say the first rule of writing is to know your audience. Do you agree?

Bill: There are many answers to this question. Work that requires the author to reach deep within his or her own experience is best written as if no audience will ever see the words. The work loses its spontaneous flow as soon as the writer becomes aware of the reader's presence. Allen Ginsberg achieved the cutting intensity of *Howl* only because he never expected to publish it. Such a work can later be edited and refined with one's readers in mind, but it can't be created with an awareness of their presence.

Pam: Does that mean you're the primary audience for your writing?

Bill: With much of my writing, the first audience is me. Writing is a way of synthesizing and integrating what I'm learning. There are times when the language I use to express this mastery is not appropriate for my eventual audience, which most of the time is front-line practitioners in substance abuse prevention and treatment. The original composition is for me; the rewriting is to refine my message for an audience.

Pam: What would be an example of this?

Bill: I recently worked on a monograph with Rita Chaney entitled, "Metaphors of Transformation: Feminine and Masculine" that explored different ideas men and women use to initiate and sustain addiction recovery. The heart of the paper was filled with straightforward language and many stories and illustrations. The opening pages of this monograph provided a sharp contrast to this clarity and simplicity of language. In writing the introductory framework, I had spilled the language of my internal musings onto the page without sufficient consciousness of my future readers. Rob Furey—one of the early reviewers of the draft paper—circled words like "androcentric," and "inductive anthropology" and scratched in the margin, "Who is your audience?"

My first drafts are generally an attempt to communicate certain ideas to myself. The purpose of editing is then to interpret the language into a form that will touch my intended readers. Rob provided a valuable service by reminding me that I had slipped into a language that would distract and decrease my readers' openness to my ideas. I had failed to make the transition between communication with self and communication with others.

Pam: So, for you, the rewriting process is the stage where your sensitivity to your audience really takes hold?

Bill: Yes. In the rewriting, the whole focus is on the clarity of my communication to the reader and how to open the reader's intellectual and emotional receptiveness to my words and ideas. To achieve the former, I refine my choice of words, images, stories, and tone. To achieve the latter, I try to be sensitive to how readers will experience my message. I try to create a sanctuary—a place of safety and comfort—in which the reader can experiment with new ideas. I've read authors who I felt were yelling at me. I try to whisper to my readers.

Research

Pam: How do you approach your research for a particular writing project?

Bill: Before beginning a formal research process, I try to start with some internal research.

Pam: I think I know what you mean by "internal research," but please describe it.

Bill: You begin by mining your experience with the topic you are addressing, reflecting carefully over what your own experience has taught you about this subject. It's important to simply spend time reflecting on the question: "What do I think about this issue?" This emotional and intellectual excavation of one's own internal landscape adds the necessary ingredients to bring the work to life. Identifying my beginning position on a subject also helps me maintain my particular focus on the subject without getting overwhelmed or lost in what others have written on the subject.

Pam: I like to write a preliminary outline—or at least a good conceptual dump—before I talk to anybody about it. That internal research also helps me identify my biases and preconceptions. That can become important to me later, particularly if it's a topic that brings out strong emotions. Do you find yourself thinking about it all the time?

Bill: I usually develop an obsession about whatever subject I'm working on. I let that subject fill my whole universe. For a period of time I filter this subject through every experience—approaching the subject from as many different angles as possible. I combine the subject with every other subject I am encountering, hoping for new breakthroughs of perception and a unique cross-fertilization of ideas.

Pam: What's your next stage, after this internal research?

Bill: With some projects, the research involves interviewing key informants until I get the needed slant for my approach. With most, the research involves a thorough review of the formal and folk literature. This stage of project development involves saturating myself in what others have written on the topic.

Pam: How do you define the difference between formal and folk literature?

Bill: Formal literature can be accessed through traditional literature searches. It can be found in libraries. It can be identified through the automated information services. Today you can call such places as the National Library of Medicine or the National Clearinghouse for Alcohol and Drug Abuse Information and they will do the beginning work for you by generating annotated bibliographies on the subjects in which you are interested. Or you can reach a wide variety of data bases through such mechanisms as Internet.

Folk literature is harder to find. Folk literature includes unpublished reports, conference papers, program descriptions, grant proposals, concept papers, self-published or small press books and curricula and other formats in which ideas have been captured on paper but not indexed for accessibility. To get these, you have to plug into networks of information junkies who collect and hang on to such hard-to-find documents.

Pam: Once you get the information from your external and internal research, how do you integrate it into your writing?

Bill: The trick is to absorb your research so completely within the writing that its presence disappears. I know I'm reading great writing when I am amazed at the depth of knowledge within a book, but was not conscious of the author's research while I was reading.

Pam: Yes, but how do you do that and still document your sources appropriately?

Bill: I try to use acknowledgement sections, prefaces, bibliographies and systems of footnoting that provide appropriate acknowledgement of my sources without distracting the reader from the story that is being told.

Pam: You also use interviews as a form of research for your writing, don't you?

Bill: I try to transport my readers to the very heart of my subject. The use of interview material can do this with remarkable intensity. Suddenly I'm not writing about AIDS, I'm letting people with AIDS talk directly to the reader. Interview material can immediately shift the treatment of a subject from the abstract to the intimate.

Pam: Do you use any special techniques that help you get the kind of material you're looking for in these interviews?

Bill: I used to think that the trick to interviewing was one of technique, but I'm becoming more convinced it's a matter of selecting the right people to interview. I try to find people who are on fire, people who have passion about the subject I'm investigating and then let them tell their story.

Approaching the Topic

Pam: What things do you think about in preparing your approach to a particular topic?

Bill: I think you always begin with a focus on the message and then explore how that message can best be conveyed. Let me give you a concrete example of this thinking process. When I had outlined the major content areas I wanted to cover in my ethics book, I sketched out such design considerations as the following:

1. *The traditions of transmitting knowledge in the field are primarily oral. The book needs to excite dialogue and discussion within the field if it is to be read.*

2. *There is a strong anti-intellectual tradition within the field—the book needs to be short and practical rather than philosophical or theoretical.*

3. *The field is broken into isolated disciplines—the book must address ethical issues within specialty roles, e.g., treatment, prevention, EAP.*

4. *The field perceives the topic of ethics as boring—the topic must be brought to life through vivid and engaging case studies.*

5. *The field is likely to be defensive of its weak efforts at ethical standards development and its past history of ethical abuses—the book must uplift rather than shame the field and the reader.*

6. *The field has a propensity for black-white thinking—the book should focus more on ethical complexities and the ethical problem-solving processes than on the presentation of simplistic ethical rules.*

Pam: You really know your audience.

Bill: If the purpose of a book is to stimulate change, it must be carefully crafted to achieve that effect. The goal of such care is not that of shallow manipulation, but the construction of one's message in a medium that personally engages the reader's involvement in the subject and enhances the reader's consideration of your ideas.

Pam: How do you sort through all the possible messages to select your message?

Bill: That sorting process is an important dimension of the writer's temperament. I think writing requires a kind of intellectual promiscuity—a capacity to embrace an enormous range of ideas in order to discover those worthy of sustained affection. You have to enter an investigation with a sense of playful adventure. You must suppress your fear of the idea and its implications and let yourself truly play with the idea—turning it over and over and rubbing it against other ideas. At some point, you have to surrender to the idea and let it take you on its natural journey. If this investigation is conducted in the freest spirit of inquiry, you really don't know the final destination. It's the joy and playfulness of this adventure that I think underlies the greatest of discoveries. When this happens in the writing process, the words move out ahead of the thoughts and I find myself speeding up in order to find out where they are going. Through this process of discovery, the message emerges on its own and presents us with a challenge of how best to introduce it to a larger audience. I often write to discover the message; I then rewrite to communicate that discovery to others.

Pam: How much does your relationship with your readers influence your approach?

Bill: My readers voluntarily consent to continue a relationship with me each time they complete and turn a page. If my language confuses, patronizes or offends, readers sense my lack of understanding and respect. If I move too far into myself and too far away from their experience and interests, readers sense my disengagement. If I take my readers' presence for granted and then return to find them, they will be gone. It's my responsibility as a writer not to lose contact with those I am writing for and to.

Writing in Tandem

Pam: How would you describe the influence of other writers on your process of selecting topics, or your approach toward those topics?

Bill: On key subjects, that influence is profound. In fact, I find myself writing in tandem with other authors, striving to achieve a kind of literary synergism. When I link my work with the work of others, the power of my voice is extended. The collective voice has a power and momentum unachievable by any single author. This collaboration of spirits is one of the ways in which writers come together and give momentum to various social movements.

Pam: What would be a current example of this?

Bill: I've been speaking and writing about abuses of power and sexual exploitation of clients within helping institutions for many years. This effort would have been impossible without an assortment of allies. There is a linked family of advocates, researchers and writers from around the world who draw strength from one another to confront such abuses. If it weren't for people like that, I wouldn't have had the courage to keep moving forward on this issue.

There really can be genuine respect and collaboration. I have deep respect for the work of Dr. LeClair Bissell and James Royce, who have written the only book other than mine on ethical issues within the substance abuse field. I respect the ground laid by their earlier work and think of my own book as a companion casebook to theirs. LeClair and I try to acknowledge and promote each other's work as we talk about resources for heightening our ethical sensitivities and ethical decision making in the field.

Chapter 5

Structure

Outlines

Pam: How much do you use outlines to guide your writing?

Bill: I outline almost everything I write before the actual writing process begins. Many of these outlines are not particularly detailed. I've found that if I get over-involved in the details of outlining, I lose the passion to write. It's almost as if solving the problem of presentation is part of the challenge of writing. If I fully resolve this problem in outlining, then I lose much of the personal challenge in the writing process.

Pam: So your outline provides only a skeleton of the work?

Bill: The outline guides my choices when I encounter forks in the road, but it doesn't take away the quality of the unknown which lies down the road. Elements of the outline represent tips of icebergs—they reveal only that dimension of my subject which I can see. When I get into writing each of these elements, I often am not sure where they will lead. The effort of writing will elicit new ideas and perceptions that would never have been born except through the disciplined attending of the writing process.

Pam: It's interesting. I may go about it in the same way, but I think of it quite differently. For me, the outline is the place where the unknown starts to reveal itself. This stage is absolutely crucial—maybe the most important part of the written work—because that's the stage in which I begin to find the structure of the work.

Bill: I noticed you said "find the structure" rather than "create the structure."

Pam: Yes. I believe that, for any given writer, a body of information contains within it a specific structure that will make the resulting document most effective and most clearly understood. Unless the writer finds that particular structure and follows it, the writer can get confused, frustrated, and blocked. I also believe that the "right" structure for a body of information differs from person to person. I think that's because no two people have the exact same combination of information, experience, and interpretation, even if there's some overlap.

Whenever I find myself blocked in a writing process, I look at the structure to see if it still fits. That's because most of my blocks seem to be about structure. If I have to go back to my collaborators and explain why I want to change the structure, then I do it. Sometimes it feels scary to re-shuffle the structure—or it feels like I'm negating the work we did before—but I've never regretted doing it.

Importance of Structure

Bill: Why is structure so important to you?

Pam: I think part of it is that I'm kind of holistic in the way I look at things: Unless I can see the whole, the parts tend not to mean very much to me. I think the reader is that way too. Even if people aren't really conscious of the structure, they can tell instinctively whether or not it all fits together. And I think, for most people, if it doesn't fit together, it doesn't get understood or retained.

Bill: What steps do you take in structuring a long document such as a manual or a long article?

Pam: The structuring process involves first breaking the source information down into smaller parts, then organizing those parts in categories, then seeing how the categories fit together—what kind of picture they make. Once I see the picture, I can see where the center is, and I know how to write about it.

Of course, the source information never comes in the same order or form that it'll ultimately appear in. There might be important little snippets in 30 different articles, and maybe a chapter of a book will have several key points, and another book will have a few good arguments—you know the drill. But when it comes time to write, I'm not going to want to have to sit there with all the articles and books spread out in front of me, trying to remember which one said what.

For me, the whole key is this: By the time I actually start writing, I want there to be as little as possible that I have to think about. I don't want to have to remember where I saw a particular quote, or wonder about the most logical order for a series of points, or wade through a long article to boil down a couple of important thoughts. I want to be free to write, as intuitively and as automatically as possible. That means it's best to have all my notes in front of me, and in order, so I can just walk down the page and write from it. That way I can concentrate on using the appropriate language, making convincing arguments, and making the text easy for the reader to float through and understand.

Sequence of Material

Bill: What criteria do you use in deciding the order in which you'll present material?

Pam: You know, I tend to think of it as a sort of automatic, intuitive process; but now that I think about it, there are some definite formulas that I tend to mix and match in ordering material.

The first is "sequential learning." I try to put myself in the place of that one reader who knows absolutely nothing about the subject. I sort of reserve a little corner of my mind where there's no knowledge of what I'm about to write about. Then I ask, from that corner, "What do I need to know first, to make the rest of it understandable?" So I put that first element into the corner, then ask myself, "What am I ready to learn next, that would build on that and get me ready for more information?", and so on until I've built it all up, block by block. This formula is very important in the introductory sections, and has to be kept in mind in structuring all the sections and sub-sections that follow.

The next formula could be called "apples and oranges." This is the point where the rather large—and sometimes rather obvious—divisions in information take place. Let's say I'm writing an article on conflict management. Maybe some of my information will be about the nature of conflict, some about the effects of letting conflict get out of hand, some about personality theory, some about brain chemistry, some about communication in general, some about effective conflict management techniques, and so on. These are the broad cuts. Within many of these large categories the information will probably fall into subcategories. Or I may get a bunch of small categories sorted out and find that they naturally group into two or three really large categories. I let the information tell me. While I'm sorting these out I don't really need to know what order I'll put them in eventually. It's like sorting socks: I can lay the individual socks out without knowing where their matches are.

Then I need to figure out the order to put the categories in—and order the information within the categories. For this I often use the "cause and effect" formula. For example, if I'm writing about the experience of children in a particular community, I might begin with the history of that community, then talk about the environmental conditions that surround families, then about the dynamics within families, then the impact of all these factors on children's emotional development, how that gets manifested in their behavior, the consequences of that behavior, possible solutions, examples of solutions that have been tried, and so on. From cause, to effect, to effect, to effect. And, of course, within each effect are new causes. That way it all gets tied together.

If I divide the structuring process into these discrete tasks, then I don't have to think consciously of too many variables at once. That leaves more room for the automatic, intuitive process that's so important to structure—where we begin to "see" the structure that's already there.´

Bill: Can you give an example of a structuring process you've undertaken in your work?

Pam: Okay. I've got a good one. Much of the content of the *Breaking the Chain* manual started out as an article for the *Prevention Forum*, written in the Fall of 1990. That was when the Illinois Institute on Drugs and Alcohol combined its annual conference with the annual convention of the National Association for Children of Alcoholics. I went there with the question, "what does the prevention field need to do to make its programs work for all kids, including kids who live with addiction?"

I attended a lot of sessions, and took notes—but I bought tapes of them too, so I could get the quotes right. I listened for anything that might be new to people in the field—that might go beyond what we always heard on the subject. In other words, I didn't want to just rehash the stats, and the "four roles" and "21 characteristics" of COAs. I wanted to address the subject at depth, but I didn't want to just say "this is a problem." I wanted to give people something they could use. I had some ideas and opinions going in, but absolutely no idea what the resulting article might look like.

What I found there—and later when I transcribed much of the information off the tapes—were some wonderful presenters with a mountain of information about kids' experiences, the effects of those experiences, things that adults can do to help, and counterproductive things that adults often do when we're trying to help. I also did a few post-conference phone interviews, and typed up these notes the same way. I don't remember how many pages of transcribed notes I ended up with—60 or 80, I think, or something ridiculous like that.

Bill: How did you deal with that much transcribed text?

Pam: Well, I started by breaking it down. I was very clever about it, if I do say so myself. I knew I was going to want to mix up all those quotes from all those different people. So I kept each speaker's quotes in a separate document, and used the word processing macro function to put the speaker's name after every paragraph of quoted text. That way I'd be able to tell who said what, even after I'd jumbled them all together. That's become a standard practice for me with material that I'm going to want to quote.

Then I printed each document out. I took the quotes one by one and decided what category of information each one belonged to—say, "core issues in alcoholic families," "problems in the helping professions," or "techniques to use with children." I wrote a code word next to each quote. Some quotes were in categories by themselves, and these I knew probably wouldn't fit into the article, but they gave some helpful background. Meanwhile I made a list of the categories I was using. Then it became time to cut and paste pieces from all the little documents into one big document—organized not according to the speakers, but according to the categories of information.

Bill: How did you decide what order to put them in?

Pam: At this point it started to dawn on me that most of these categories fell logically into two groups.   The first had to do with things that we in the prevention field should take into account in order to understand children who live with addiction.   The second had to do with things we needed to keep in mind in designing programs, working with kids, and educating our communities.   It made sense, and answered that all-important question, "so what do I **do** with all this?"   I had two major groups of information, and each group had seven points under it—each point being one of those categories of information I'd identified early in the process.

Bill: You mentioned seeing a picture of the information and finding its center.   Did this process help you find the center?

Pam: It really did—at least where the center was at the time.   The picture turned out to be sort of a forked tree-trunk, with those two groups of recommendations branching out.   The trunk itself was the critical importance of making our programs work for all children.   Children who live with addiction have experiences that are different in many ways from what we'd always thought of as "mainstream" family life, and the traditional prevention techniques don't fit that experience.   I had a wonderful long quote from Cathleen Brooks, a story that really brought that point home, both logically and emotionally.   I used that quote to introduce the article.

The rest was fairly simple.   The word processing package we use allows us to have two documents open at once, and switch back and forth from screen to screen.   I kept the huge document with notes in one screen, and started writing in the other, using my printed copy of the notes as a general guide.   Every time I wanted to throw in a quote, I just switched screens, swooped up the appropriate quote, and carried it over to my document in progress.   I could tell who was speaking by the name in parentheses at the end, which I modified to fit the journalistic style that the whole thing was following.

Bill: How did the structure change later, when you added to the information to make *Breaking the Chain*?

Pam: We were lucky enough to get Cathleen Brooks to act as guest editor for that manual.   She provided an important focus—three things that adults need to keep in mind when working with children from addicted families: 1) Listen, rather than talk; 2) Learn and understand what these children experience and how it shapes their survival systems; and 3) Understand that their behavior makes sense in the context of their home experience. That became the new tree trunk, and it added meaning to all the branches. We also kept Cathleen's quote and set it off at the very beginning of the manual.

Structure Under Time Pressure

Bill: That sounds like a rewarding process, but a very long one. How do you find the structure when you don't have much time?

Pam: I really had that tested out a few months later, when I coordinated the recording for some focus groups at the conference, "Latinos, Drugs, and HIV/AIDS." Each focus group was assigned a different set of questions to discuss. They all met simultaneously, and each one had its own recorder who took copious notes on a legal pad. After the session was done, I had just a few hours to go through all their notes, structure them, and come up with a two-page report on the combined results. All I needed was a laptop, a printer, and a quiet space.

First I read through their rough notes a couple of times. Then I transferred their major points onto the laptop in abbreviated form, but in no particular order—no more than one line per point—and printed it out. That way I could see it all on one or two pages instead of flipping through six notebooks. Then I assigned categories to the points. I came up with a two-letter code for each category and wrote those two-letter codes in the margins.

When I was done with that, I simply wrote from the coded sheet. The whole process took just a few hours, and we had printed copies for the final plenary session. Because I'd coded and ordered the information, I was able to reflect all the major points brought up in all six sessions—and do it in a structure that made sense.

Bill: Did you learn anything from having to do the structuring process so quickly?

Pam: Yes! I learned—too late for that project—that I should always have a set of colored pencils or marking pens available for coding pieces of information. Now I just assign colors to different categories of information. For every line or paragraph in that category, I draw a colored line down the left-hand margin. When it's time to write, or cut and paste my notes, I just do it by color codes. It makes it much faster and takes less brain power.

Bill: It sounds as if the word processing technology is important in your structuring processes.

Pam: It really is. I'm sure that even without using computers I'd find a way, but the technology makes it a lot easier and a lot quicker. I love being able to pirate text from one screen and pull it into another—and I understand that some word processing programs have many more screens. I love being able to cut and paste. The whole point of word processing is to allow us to do things over and over until we get them right.

Bill: Then I presume you do your drafts of text on the computer too.

Pam: Always! I've just been using them too long. It makes me nuts even to try doing something longhand. I can do it, but it always feels like I'm wasting time. The computer is so much more alive, in a way. What I write can grow and change as my thoughts grow and change.

Bill: I've heard writers say that the structural aspect of writing gives them some trouble because they're not what they call "structured people." Do you consider yourself a "structured person"?

Pam: Good Lord, no! I mean, given a body of information—in any setting— I'll almost compulsively look for structure in it. But in my own actions I'm not particularly "structured," whatever that is. I love thinking of systems and strategies for organizing life, but I have very little interest in following them, and tend to abandon them immediately. And I'm not particularly fond of structure imposed from outside, although I've gotten pretty good at coping with it (or getting around it gracefully). It's part of basic survival.

With all the things I'm involved in these days I'm scheduled every minute of the week, but nothing would please me more than to have several days—or several weeks—with no itinerary whatsoever. Maybe that's why I like to find structure in the information I deal with. As long as the inside of my head is in order, I can live comfortably in a world where one trips over things.

Bill: I think it's important that we pay this much attention to the process that takes place before the actual writing. People think writing is what we do when we sit down in front of the computer. It's a lot more involved than that. Water heats for a long time and then boils suddenly. That's what happens with my writing. What I primarily do is read, observe, ask questions, listen and think. I'm writing when I'm doing any of these things. Putting the words on paper is just the condensation of these activities. The words may suddenly boil out, but they have been cooking for a long time.

Chapter 6

The Process of Writing

Original Composition

Pam: Describe how you experience the process of original composition.

Bill: Sometimes I write like a painter, choosing and placing each word as carefully as if I were placing paint on a canvas. Then there are times I sculpt, producing a large mass of writing that must then be chipped away to reveal my final product.

Pam: There's a tendency among some writers to describe composition in terms of pain. How would you explain that?

Bill: I don't know. Writers have always talked about writing in these terms. Hemingway and Mailer talked about writing as boxing. Tolstoy talked about leaving one's flesh in the ink pot. Churchill compared writing a book to a long painful illness. Conrad and Binet compared their writing to difficult births. Hundreds of others speak of writing in metaphors of sweat and blood. No one would be drawn to writing if they only listened to such words. What lies behind the rhetoric of blood and sweat are experiences of awe and ecstacy within the creative process. These moments of stunning intensity more than make up for the frustration and strain that precede and follow them.

Pam: When you start a writing project, how much conscious thought goes into your selection of language and tone?

Bill: I don't spend a lot of conscious time on language and tone. I do try to work out in the early pages the degree of formality or informality with which I wish to conduct my dialogue with the reader. This early tone becomes the standard by which I judge the rest of the work for consistency. In the rewriting, I target word selection and sentence construction that are incongruent with this desired tone.

Pam: I think of finding the right tone as—more than anything else—a balancing act. That's why absolute rules can get in the way more than they help.

Bill: What are you balancing?

Pam: Lots of things. For one thing, the right and left hemispheres of the brain—intuition and logic, emotion and detachment, the writer and the editor. There also has to be a balance of excitement and calm, or the reader either falls asleep or fails to assimilate what I'm writing. I have to balance my desire for the reader's interest with my desire to be truthful. And as we were talking about before, I have to balance the need to be brief with the need to promote understanding.

There's another balancing act going on, too, and it has to do with the sound of the words themselves. There's the balance of sound against silence, the cadence of the words. And I have to balance my desire for a graceful cadence with my desire to pick words that will say what I mean and be easy to understand.

The Use of Words and Imagery

Bill: Do you think your musical background has an effect on your choice of words?

Pam: Definitely. When I'm writing I tend to automatically go for rhythmic combinations of words—not necessarily iambic pentameter or anything, but words where there's sort of a dance in the way they fall together. I also tend to go for alliteration and assonance, and sort of line those things up with the rhythm.

I think these things make it easier on the reader. People may not be paying conscious attention to the musical elements of good writing, but I know they get more pleasure from it if those elements have been done with care. And the rhythm forms a sort of momentum, pulling the reader forward through the text. It's like when I'm dancing: If the song has a lot of good sub-rhythms, I'll move a lot more, but it'll seem to take a lot less energy. It's the same thing with good writing. Of course there's a danger there.

Bill: The danger of compromising something else?

Pam: Yes. Maybe compromising meaning, or brevity, or understandability, or visual imagery. That's why it would be a mistake to try to stick to a formula for making the words sound good. It can't be something I do mechanically.

Bill: Do you do it unconsciously?

Pam: Sometimes. Sometimes I'll also be conscious of weighing different ways of saying something, and some of them will sound better than the others. Instinct will usually tell me which ones to choose, and I do it more-or-less automatically.

It's like driving. When I'm coming around a curve and I see that there's somebody in the road ahead, I don't sit there and say to myself, "Let's see. There's somebody in the road. If I accelerate, I'll smoosh him. If I brake, I won't smoosh him, but if there's anybody close behind me they might smoosh me. Let's see. I wonder if there's anybody behind me . . ." It doesn't even make it to the word stage. My body just glances in the rear-view mirror and hits the brake.

Bill: Do you think that comes from having done it so much?

Pam: Partly. It's partly that and it's partly a willingness to let go and listen to my intuition. If I couldn't do that, writing would be much more difficult, no matter how smart I was. It would be like filling out tax forms or something. I'd put it off forever.

Bill: Do you also use imagery and metaphor to enhance this concrete understanding?

Pam: I do, but I'm very much aware of the need to be careful with metaphor. If the individual image or metaphor is something that's almost universally understood, then it'll probably enhance understanding. If it's just my flight of fancy, though, it'll probably get in the way. An example of one that I thought worked well was at the beginning of the "Cultural Traditions" chapter of *Tools for Transformation*. I wrote, "Cultural traditions exist for many reasons. They keep us rooted, but they also point out where the sky is."

Of course, that's not true in any literal sense. But most people who read that will interpret it in terms of stability and high aspirations. The difference is that it might evoke an emotional response that an objective discussion of stability and high aspirations wouldn't evoke. You've heard the old saying, "Don't tell me: Show me." The better we use visual imagery, the more it pulls the reader into the experience—and the experience into the reader.

They say we all have these screening systems in our heads, where we sift through all the words we hear, and sort them logically. Anything we can dismiss or just dismantle, we probably will, unless we perceive it as being useful to us. But imagery is like another language that's too fine to get caught in that net. It just passes through, and goes in much deeper. Have you ever seen a movie—and you don't even have to have liked it very well—but you find that two days later the images are still vivid in your head? They got in there. They got past your screening system.

Bill: What kinds of images and metaphors do and don't work for you?

Pam: Sometimes simile doesn't work for me. It can feel awkward and forced for me to say that something is "like" something else. Robert Frost wrote that "The fog comes in on little cat feet." If he'd written "The fog is like a cat," nobody would have read it. Of course, there are exceptions. I've seen some highly effective use of simile.

I also don't do well with really lofty, dramatic metaphors. I like to go for a more mixed approach—one foot in poetry and one foot in the Campbell's Soup can. I think of a song by Thomas Dolby, on his "Astronauts and Heretics" album. It's a love song, but it's full of the most wonderfully inappropriate similes, like "Once in a while a girl comes along who opens your heart like a Spam tin." And in his refrain he says "I'm sinking like a bug on a peach." How romantic. It really gets your attention.

I think the thing I do most often and most effortlessly is use verbs that, in context, become metaphorical. For example, instead of talking about "separating" one experience or emotion from another, I might talk about "untangling" them. Or in one article, instead of saying that a particular problem was a "fact of human life," I wrote that it was a problem that "our species cannot shake." Now if I were writing for people with certain kinds of cognitive disabilities, I probably wouldn't use offbeat verbs or metaphor of any kind. But for general audiences, I think it's okay to throw a few of these in, especially if they're common colloquial terms. They make the text more interesting and more accessible—and actually more concrete, in a weird sort of way.

The Power and Potential Misuse of Words and Imagery

Pam: What do writers need to be careful about in selecting words and imagery?

Bill: I've come to increasingly appreciate the power of words and the ways in which they can be used and abused. Many writers bring not only a love of words, but a respect for the words and the images they convey. Words and metaphors can have enormous power. They can create new breakthroughs in perception. They can stir deep emotion. They can call us to action. It's their very power that must caution us in their use. Dire consequences can flow from our loss of specificity in the use of language and metaphor.

Pam: What's an example of that?

Bill: Language can be abused through laziness or conscious manipulation. We all lose when the language of our discourse is diluted or distorted either through misuse or overuse. There are many examples in which our lack of precision with words, our exploitation of words, or misuse of a metaphor has hurt the field.

Our social policies toward illicit drug use for the past two decades have been organized around the metaphor of war. The language of this period has been the language of battle. Language, images, and metaphors that are extreme generate responses that are excessive. Words have power. Words pull us toward their inherent meaning. If we use the metaphor of war, the actions that emerge from this metaphor will inevitably produce conflict and aggression. If we use war as a metaphor to approach anything, we will eventually draw blood. The blood that is staining American streets today is blood that is being shed as a result of this war.

Wars are always fought against real people. Wars to "stamp out" drugs always end up stamping out people. "Zero tolerance" for drugs inevitably is converted into zero tolerance for certain classes of people. I believe the highly celebrated war on drugs of the 1980's was a euphemism for this culture's undeclared war on young Black men. We are reaping the inextricable logic of our metaphor. It's time for a new metaphor!

Pam: Talking about it as a war also automatically directed people's attention—and the lion's share of the money—toward interdiction, rather than toward prevention and treatment. This happened despite the fact that interdiction is far more costly and has a much lower ratio of success than prevention or treatment. But if we think of ourselves as being "at war," it would feel far less noble to admit that the physical "war on drugs" is a war we can't ever win or even make significant headway in, no matter how much money we throw at it. But if we could make that admission, we'd realize the real problems are not "enemies" that can be singled out and eradicated. The real problems run through our entire society. We need to direct the money toward the more effective prevention and treatment strategies that desperately need it.

What are some other words or images that have been abused in the addiction treatment field?

Bill: There are words like "disease" that have been powerful metaphors around which both social policies and thousands of individual recoveries have been organized. And yet the deification of this word within the field has lead to rhetorical debates in which the metaphor is either defended or attacked based on scientific truthfulness, rather than on its utility as an organizing metaphor. Both sides in this debate can do potential harm.

The disease-bashing that is now in vogue denies the usefulness of this concept in the personal transformation of thousands of addicted people and their family members. The disease-bashers, by attacking the legitimacy and over-application of the disease concept, risk discarding both the potential scientific and metaphorical utility of the concept. They are saying that the truth that has transformed a million lives is a lie. The rigid disease-defenders, by mistaking their metaphorical truth for scientific reality, deny other people access to alternative metaphors that may be more culturally and personally helpful in their movement from addiction to recovery.

We're abusing words and ideas with such abandon in some areas of the field that we're running out of words that have meaning. The over-extension of the concept of co-dependency has all but destroyed the clinical utility of this concept. Critics are justifiably challenging that if co-dependency is everything, then it's nothing.

We need language that has precision and metaphors that are consistent with our goals and our values. Writers bear a responsibility to create that precision to the best of their ability and to avoid weakening or destroying the utility of our metaphors through misapplication or overuse.

Writing Style

Pam: How would you describe your own writing style?

Bill: I think most seasoned writers—particularly writers of non-fiction—have little awareness of style. They write the way they write—and then try to describe in interviews like this what it is they do—explanations that may have little to do with their writing process.

The only thing I'm conscious of in a book like *Culture*, for example, is the constant shift from a theoretical construct to a vivid illustration that makes that construct come alive. One of my writing mottoes is: minimize theory, maximize detail. I try to sustain an acute awareness of my reader as I shift from the theoretical to the practical, from logical appeal to emotional connection. What I'm seeking is a style that allows the reader to simultaneously think and feel, a fusion between analytical thinking and affective experience.

What about you? Do you find yourself thinking consciously about the style in which you're writing?

Pam: I think I'm very deliberate about style simply because I've done most of my writing on assignment by organizations or publications. I have to be quite conscious of the style, because the people who have assigned these projects usually have a specific style in mind—although many people don't know how to articulate it. But I've written in many styles, usually consciously, and usually to fit the assignment.

When I don't feel any external constraints—and I guess that would just be for my personal writing—I tend to write with a sort of mixed style—long and short sentences interspersed; big words, simple words, and slang; and as much rhythmic movement and sound quality as I can fit without distorting the meaning. This is the style I use in writing letters to friends, or just describing a concept or experience.

I used to be afraid that trying to write more simply would make my writing more clunky, less graceful. But in the past year or so I've discovered a style that's as simple and as colloquial as possible, but it flows smoothly. I think it was just a matter of getting used to using simpler words and shorter sentences.

Writing as Storytelling

Pam: When you're writing something, do you keep a particular reader in mind?

Bill: I keep many specific reader's in mind. What I try to do is read my work through the experience of people with different levels of experience in the field, who bring different perspectives of gender or ethnicity, who work in different modalities and who work in very diverse environments. I think a guiding motif in the construction of anecdote and illustration is: honor the diversity of your reader. Through the details of your storytelling, you can let each of them know you are aware of their existence and the importance of their contribution.

Pam: I really like the use of stories and anecdotes in your books and monographs. There are a lot of them, and they're woven in very nicely.

Bill: Stories open the emotional receptiveness of the reader, preparing the groundwork for what educators have long called the "teachable moment"—an openness to learning, loving, healing, emerging.

Pam: I also think individual examples help people relate. Why does the public respond more strongly to the story about one little boy who's been killed than to the horrifying statistics about all the children who've been killed? I don't think we're equipped to identify with more than one person at once—and I think that inability is there to keep us from going crazy. But unless we identify, we don't understand what it all means to us as human beings.

Where do the stories come from?

Bill: I think as a writer you have to use your own life and the lives of those around you as a laboratory. I mine experiences for meaning. I'm always prospecting for ideas and stories that can be used to transmit ideas. I start with the local, the particular, the personal and then extract from that what seems to be universal. I try to always ask myself, "What can this little detail tell us about the big picture?" I think all the ultimate issues of the universe get played out within the microcosms of our individual stories. It's the way each of us knowingly or unknowingly effects history. Linking the particular to the universal is the essence of great writing. The great writers find ways to transmit the most abstract and global issues through the story of a single human life.

Pam: We need Studs Terkels in our field, to capture the stories.

Bill: Yes, we do. There are yet-to-be-born writers who aren't naturally drawn to putting words on paper. They write not with pen and paper, but out of the action of their daily lives. Writers can give added meaning to the lives of such people by passing on their experiences to new generations of explorers. From this perspective, the function of the writer within the field is a clerical one. We are scribes whose job it is to capture and interpret the words of our people (clients, service providers and citizens). Our job is to help all of them tell their stories.

Pam: Do you use special techniques in relating these stories?

Bill: I've tried to study the work of writers who spring from oral cultures to master the techniques of transmitting stories on paper. My reading of African-American and Native American writers has been particularly instructive in helping me explore how to create written work out of primarily oral traditions. These writers have had to find a way to translate the sounds and the rhythms of their cultures into words and sentences. In oral cultures, words are lyrics whose meaning can only be fully understood through the subtlety of tone, pitch, and pace and a surrounding choreography of gesture, movement and place. One of my favorite poets is Langston Hughes—you can feel the blues and feel the jazz in his poems, you can feel Harlem and feel the Mississippi River. To create such vivid experience through the placement of words on paper is a remarkable achievement.

What one learns from writers from oral cultures is how to sharpen one's senses. Aspiring writers must learn to expand their ability to consciously absorb and depict the world through the senses. I say consciously because they must be able to let the awareness of seeing, hearing, smelling, tasting, touching come through in their writing. The need for this quality is obvious in fiction writers, but it's equally important for non-fiction writers. My admonition to the aspiring writer is: bring even the most abstract of subjects to your readers through their senses. Take the most ethereal of subjects and let your reader taste it, and hear it, and smell it, and feel its touch.

Conquering Grammarphobia

Pam: I've known many people who had a lot to say—from their own and others' experience—but who discounted their ability to write because they were poor spellers or because their grammar wasn't the best. What would you say to somebody like that?

Bill: The best way to learn to write is to write. You just have to do it. You have to get your experience and your message on paper. The message is the most important focus. The technical aspects of writing can be learned, polished and refined, and many of us will always need computers that spell check and skillful editors and proof readers. But the best technical skills in the world are impotent if you don't have anything of importance to say. If you have something to say, struggling to master the craft of writing is worth the effort.

Pam: It's frustrating for writers who have problems with grammar, because there's so much about the English language that's illogical. It would be one thing if the rules all made sense and were applied more consistently, as they are in Spanish or French. But they're not. It's a patchwork language, put together from widely different language traditions. Unfortunately, learning its nuances is often a matter of just memorizing the rules and all the exceptions.

Do you have any tips for mastering grammar that could help writers who are intimidated by their lack of technical skill?

Bill: Learning the correct use of language is cumulative. You master it one tiny lesson at a time in the same way a beautiful brick home is built one brick at a time. I think the essence of writing in English is captured in Strunk and White's little book, *The Elements of Style*. My tip for the technically intimidated writer is to read this book—AGAIN AND AGAIN—fully absorbing one new lesson with each reading.

Pam: I agree. And after Strunk and White, it's time to get Theodore Bernstein's *The Careful Writer*. That one's in dictionary form, and gives all the subtle nuances of what words mean, how they're used, the prepositions they take, and the differences between words that are often thought to be interchangeable.

I guess the point is that everyone who knows grammar had to memorize it at some point. It's not something people were born with, and it's not a exclusive club that only certain people can join. It may be easier to learn it as a child—when you have no idea how much more interesting other things can be—but learning it as an adult has its advantages too. It's a key that makes it possible for your ideas to enter any door—gives them complete mobility. When editors and readers are no longer distracted or confused by the grammatical problems, the written work gains considerable power.

Challenges of Brevity

Bill: When it comes to the craft itself, what's your greatest challenge at this stage of your development as a writer?

Pam: Trying not to write too long. That's important to me for a number of reasons. First, making things concise is something we're emphasizing at PRC and Prevention First as a whole—for training manuals and other publications. The field has less and less time to read, and more and more things we need to read about. Everybody's under stress, and nobody has time to wade through long documents. People need things that are short, concrete, and action oriented. I think learning to write shorter is also an excellent discipline for me.

Bill: What factors make that difficult for you now?

Pam: I don't think I've always shown enough faith in the readers—faith that they'll understand what I'm saying even if I don't explain it completely. It's kind of like your caution against doing too much for the reader. I have this tremendous urge to give people all the information they might possibly need. But I have to fight that urge and learn to trust.

One more challenge: If I know a document's going to be read by people at varying levels of knowledge and comprehension, then I sometimes tend to overdo it. I want to include all the basic stuff for the beginners, and the advanced stuff for the old pros. I couldn't keep doing that, though. I think I cheated both ends of the spectrum when I tried to be all things to all people. So we're narrowing our focus.

Bill: How are you narrowing your focus?

Pam: One way is just to do it—take some things out of the outline and set limits on what the document can cover. Another way is to be more specific in targeting audiences, and not try to write things that will work for such a broad spectrum of people.

Another way of narrowing it is to set limits on how deep the document will go in addressing its topic. That's the hardest for me, because by nature I always want to understand things at depth. Don't just tell me what to do; tell me why—what's behind it, what's underneath it, what it feels like, and what it all means. I've finally accepted the fact that not everybody wants that much information. And what if people really do need that much information? If they get stalled and give up halfway through it, who am I helping? Nobody!

Bill: Is it kind of disheartening, the idea of excluding information that you believe people need to know?

Pam: Well, it was for a while. At first I saw it as the difference between an in-depth approach and a cookbook. But then I thought of another way of looking at it. Now I think of it as the difference between prose and poetry. I'd been going at it as if it were prose—straight exposition—and I needed to think a little more like a poet. It's in poetry that those gaps that you mentioned occur, those gaps that the reader completes.

Think of a poem you really like. It doesn't provide all the information there is to provide about its subject, but its impact is much stronger. The reader understands on a deeper level than if the whole thing were laid out. The poet needs to lead readers up to the edge of the chasm, give them enough momentum to get across, and be waiting for them when they land—but the leap itself is up to the reader. That's where the exhilaration comes from. It's from making that leap. And what makes the leap possible? The fact that the poet trusts the reader!

Bill: Does this mean PRC will be coming out with training manuals that rhyme?

Pam: Don't tempt me! I'm famous for my Epic Limericks!

But seriously, I'm not sure how it'll play out in the things I write. The closest I've ever come to doing this was in *Tools for Transformation* and *Increase the Peace*, where I was very much aware of the need to make them simple and concrete. They ended up being more creative. I must have felt freed of my urge to make things comprehensive.

I can think of examples in other people's writing. Hugh Prather's *Notes on Love and Courage* immediately comes to mind, although it's a completely different type of document. But it's that ability—and willingness—to boil things down to their essence and leave them there, surrounded by silence. It's very powerful.

Bill: Are there any other methods of eliminating excess material that you've found useful?

Pam: Yes. Probably one of the most important devices I've run into is the concept of "horse latitudes."

Bill: Horse latitudes?

Pam: There was a song by that name on an old Doors album—I think it was *Strange Days*. It was about a place out on the ocean, somewhere near the equator, where the trade winds died down. The old sailing ships would get to that place and they'd get "becalmed"—there was no wind, no currents, so they couldn't go anywhere. They'd start to run out of food and fresh water, and still no wind. So they finally had to start throwing overboard whatever they could do without—and in many cases that meant the horses.

Now in almost every writing project there seems to come a point when I'm running out of time, and it becomes clear that I can't include everything I want to include and still make my deadline and have a cohesive product. So I tell myself it's time to start throwing the horses overboard—time to look for the stuff I can get along without. It's a horrible image, but maybe that's appropriate. There's always a sense of loss when we have to modify our ambitions and do what an old editor of mine used to suggest—"dwell in the realm of the possible."

Bill: I think that's something most writers have to confront at some point. Does it make it easier when you turn it into a regular ritual like that?

Pam: It does. It sort of legitimatizes it. It's no longer, "Uh-oh, I goofed. I put too much stuff in the outline." Instead it's just another routine part of the writing process. And what I've discovered is that the earlier I do it, the less anxiety I have to deal with. For one thing, the deadline's farther away. But in general, the earlier in the process I cut something out of the outline, the more naturally and easily the rest of the outline "grows" back together over the hole.

Usually—almost always—the document ends up being the better for it. But the process is always a little scary. Part of it is just trusting that, if something really needs to be said, it will be said. And if I don't get a chance to say it, somebody else will.

When To Kill a Writing Project

Pam: What happens when you get lost in the middle of a project or the project loses steam?

Bill: Sometimes projects just need more time to mature. In this case, they can often be revived at a later date. Some projects, however, never make the transition from the beauty of the idea to the execution on paper. When such projects stumble horribly, some of them need to be ended. It's a form of literary mercy killing. I generally ask myself two questions when a project seems to be floundering: 1) will the completion of this project make a significant contribution to the field?, and 2) will I feel good about being the author of this product? When the answers are "NO!" it's time to kill the project.

When I skim through my unpublished—complete and incomplete—writing, I can find pieces that are technically well written but lack value because I failed to find a way to experience the subject. They are literary skeletons that lack breath and spirit. They deserve to remain unpublished. There's enough dead writing already cluttering up the world.

Pam: When do you make that decision?

Bill: Sometimes I make the decision early: a project simply doesn't get off the ground. Other times, I get well into a project when I discover that something's missing. My loss of energy to work on the project usually is my cue that the project needs to be terminated or moved into hibernation until I get a revived vision of it.

Pam: Does that mean that all the time you spent on the project has been wasted?

Bill: No. The project may be stopped but there are ideas within the project that may have great value. One must be very careful about discarding ideas.

I have ideas that suddenly appear and worm their way into my current writing projects. They don't belong there and must eventually be edited out, but their intrusiveness is often the seed of a future paper or book. Some writing projects generate their own children, some of whom could grow up to change the world. You never know. Within today's discarded project may be the germ of your greatest contribution.

Pam: That makes an argument for patience. We have to have the patience to wait until we know what that particular idea means, we have enough information to back it, and the time is right to introduce it.

Rewriting

Pam: How are the processes of original composition and rewriting different for you?

Bill: The psychology of original composition is very different from that of rewriting and editing. In my composition process, I'm trying to reach that state of flow where the words have a life of their own and tell their own story. The words come from me, but from sources so deep that they remain a mystery. Rewriting, in contrast, is a very conscious process. Composition is a kind of spiritual seizure; rewriting is sweat and discipline. The former is the exuberant child; the latter is the hypercritical parent. If the internal critic can't be shut off for original composition, it will check our ability to tell the truth. This very critic must then be brought to life to polish one's rough work into completed form. Rewriting must be as heartless as the raw composition is passionate. Editing requires the capacity to destroy with cold objectivity that which is inferior within one's own creations.

Writing combines two very different processes: unrestrained creation and critical self-appraisal. If we can't force a separation between these two functions, each will destroy the other. If creation overwhelms self-appraisal, we spew out work, good and bad, on a readership who may not have the patience to find our pearls in the sand. If self-appraisal overwhelms creation, we become paralyzed or produce work that is cold and constrained. It's the separation and balance of these two functions that creates great writing.

The processes of original composition and rewriting are also experienced very differently by the writer. The pleasure in rewriting is not this spiritual release of the message on paper; it's the pleasure of precision achieved by consciously reviewing the selection and placement of every single word and sentence.

Pam: There may be exceptions to that separation of processes. I tend to write and rewrite all at once, routinely, and I feel no difficulty or discomfort in switching back and forth from the unrestrained writer to the critic. I make those switches rapidly and frequently, and with no conscious deliberation. I just sort of shift back and forth as the situation suggests. Of course, I also edit and rewrite several times after that first session.

That may be why I find it so much easier to compose on the computer. My internal editor can jump in any time and change what I've written, then my writer can start writing again immediately. Before the editor has stopped editing, the writer is working on the next thought, and vice-versa. If I only have a paper and pen, I feel stifled, constricted.

Bill: That is a remarkable difference in our writing styles. I wonder if there are any gender influences at work here.

Pam: It may or may not have something to do with our difference in gender. I've read that women's brains have a lot more electrical impulses jumping back and forth between the left and right hemispheres—more communication between the rational and creative functions. This would make sense, given the difference in the complexity of social expectations that are placed on developing girls and boys. It would be interesting to look at male and female writers and see what percentage of each group combines those two functions, and what percentage keeps them separate.

When you do get to the rewriting phase, how much do you actually rewrite?

Bill: I've increased the effort that goes into rewriting over the course of my writing career. I think I'm just beginning to fully understand this dimension of writing. One of the best books that really captures the essence of the drafting, redrafting and polishing aspects of writing is Howard Becker's *Writing for Social Scientists*. For a long time I had what he depicts as the college view of writing—something written one time the day before it's due. I thought composing first drafts was writing and that great writers simply created first drafts of higher quality than us common folk. I had no idea what it was like to take a product through multiple evolutions of structure and language. What I thought was the end of writing was only the beginning. Becker provides a very realistic description of what comes after the first draft—knowledge it took me years to acquire on my own. I'm slowly learning that the ability to read with that critical eye and return again and again to polish my work is the very essence of writing.

Pam: Have you broken down the various functions you perform in rewriting?

Bill: Episodes of revising have multiple targets: correcting problems of structure, clarifying one's meaning, polishing language, and correcting problems of presentation such as spelling and grammar. I have a tendency to overwrite, so my first edit is aimed at achieving greater condensation and precision. I delete unnecessary words, sentences and paragraphs; and then I go through again to shorten words, sentences, and paragraphs.

Pam: Are there any special techniques you use in rewriting?

Bill: I often step back in the revision process and ask myself how one of my heroes might view a particular problem or state a particular point. Some of these people I've read so thoroughly—or studied the idiosyncracies of their thought and speech so completely—that I really do think I can project what they would think and say. Through such mental projection, I have an unlimited supply of consultants to assist me in my thinking and my writing.

Pam: What a good idea! I'm going to try that.

Bill: I also try to edit my work through a variety of senses. I review sentences and paragraphs for the feelings they evoke. I read them aloud to test their sound and rhythm. Sometimes I find a section of my work that says what I want to say but its feel and sound don't match the effect I want the words to have on the reader. I often rewrite by ear to achieve rhythm. When I'm at my best, there's an emotional rhythm that emerges in my writing. This emotional rhythm can either enhance or undermine my message. I try to revise with a consciousness of this rhythm. Sometimes a sentence needs a changed word, or a paragraph needs a changed sentence, not to complete its meaning but to achieve the right pulse beat.

Pam: That's an important process for me too, but I find that it's easiest if I start it with the first draft. It actually eases the original flow of words if they come out in a way that pleases my sense of rhythm.

What other senses seem to help you in the rewriting process?

Bill: I also edit visually. I like to use titles and subtitles, paragraphing, indentations, bulleted lists, and other devices to help my reader's eyes move through the text. I try to surround units of my words with white space. White space frames and softens my writing, making it more digestible. White space is a crucial feature to non-fiction writing.

Pam: I also value white space very highly. But that sometimes brings me into conflict with the value of covering the material on as few pages as possible—a value that can be important when funds are scarce. I find it quite a struggle to balance those two values.

Do you rewrite as you finish each chapter or section, or return to rewrite the entire work at a later time?

Bill: Timing is an important aspect of rewriting for me. I have to let the passion out of which I composed the first draft cool before I can return to judge it. I need to let enough time pass that I can come back and revisit the work as a stranger rather than as a parent.

Pam: Are you ever satisfied with your finished products?

Bill: I would have new revisions today for every piece of work I've ever published. I'm satisfied with most of my works but every page of each could be improved. I'm one of those writers who continues to make final edits as they take pages from my hands to the printer.

Pam: I've had that tendency too, but then I find that I keep wanting to make more edits after it's already been printed. I've instituted a policy that goes into effect as soon as something I've written comes back from the printer. Anybody who points out a typo or another kind of error in it has to pay me $10. It really cuts down on those post-printing pangs of regret.

Do you ever re-read your works after they've been published?

Bill: Only under certain circumstances. I re-read some of my material to recall what I discovered and wrote on a particular topic. When I feel low energy in my writing or feel I've lost touch with my writing self, I go back and re-read some of my published work. It reminds me what the process is all about—getting the product out—and it helps me re-establish an emotional connection to my writing. I can sometimes pick up a lost rhythm in my writing by reading previous work. This is a process similar to that used by slumping athletes who recapture their form by viewing videotape of their top performances.

Writing Rooms, Writing Rituals and Writing Tools

Pam: The literature about writers and writing is filled with allusions to "the writing room." Do you have a special place where you write?

Bill: I do a lot of my writing while I'm traveling, but I do have my own special writing room. I think each writer needs a sacred place—what Joseph Campbell called a "place of creative incubation." Each writer must find or create that unique environment that elicits the best within them. Maya Angelou, for example, rents a sparse hotel room with nothing in it but a Bible and a dictionary. In contrast, my writing room is filled to the brim with books, sculptures, photographs, and items from my many collections. When I go into that room to write, remnants of all my favorite people and places are there to nurture me. There is my strange collection of antiques and artifacts that keep me sensitized to history. The juxtaposition of modern computers sitting on century-old oak library tables blends old and new. There are objects of art and books from many cultures reminding me how diverse my audience is. There are ceremonial masks, voodoo dolls (gifts from loved ones), patent medicine bottles, wooden boxes, carvings, sculptures, bells, animal skulls, mineral specimens, shells, dried seedpods, bird nests, bird feathers, dried flowers, pictures of my Japanese garden and stained glass windows. Books fill the walls floor to ceiling There are special places for the books of my heroes and heroines—they must be close by in case I need to be reminded of their presence or need to consult them. The whole place looks likes a collision between a library and a museum storage room. Other writers couldn't stand it; for me, it's perfect! It has a cave-like feel that I often metaphorically think of as the womb out of which my writing is born.

How about you? What kind of writing atmosphere is best for you?

Pam: I like to write—or at least to start a project—in an atmosphere that's as free of clutter as possible. Of course, that's not easy, given the number of things going on in my life. There's so much clutter, and only so many places to put it before it kind of seeps out and comes creeping into the writing room—that's how it seems sometimes, anyway. So I've learned to tune out my environment and concentrate no matter what. When I'm at work, I have a V-shaped desk, which is wonderful. I can keep one half completely messy, and the other half pristine. I put my source materials and outlines on the clean half, so I can look only in that direction and pretend the other half looks the same. At home, I write in my dining room—particularly in the winter, because that's the only room that's warm enough. I sit in a comfortable chair, with the keyboard on my lap. I've built a little nest of furniture around me, so I can have source materials, outlines, and drafts where I can see them and grab them.

How would you describe your writing rituals?

Bill: There are rituals of time. People think writing is when I sit down in front of my computer, but the fact is I'm writing most of the time. When I'm thinking, I'm writing. When my thinking gets to critical mass, I have this need to catch what comes out on paper. It's sort of like popcorn overflowing the pot. I scramble for notebooks or scraps of paper to catch the overflow.

I do a lot of thinking and note-taking during the hours I spend in travel related to my training activities. I think my car is an idea chamber—I use it a lot for periods of sustained thinking. It works great until I return to consciousness, oblivious to where my vehicle and I are currently located.

There are also rituals of atmosphere. Ideas can be born within two very different environments. Some ideas are born amid the noisy chaos of the most frenetic environments. Suddenly visible amid the swirl of interaction and activity is the pearl of an idea of uncommon value. The birth of such an idea requires the synergy of relationship, the fuel of connecting or clashing spirits. The process of emergence for other ideas is so fragile that the slightest noise or movement would doom their birth. These ideas emerge from the deepest silence within the self. To create works of depth, the writer must explore one or both of these worlds. I try to match the sounds in my writing environments with the nature of my writing. Some of my writing I prefer to do in silence; other types of writing I prefer classical music in the background. I select music whose tone and pace matches that which I'm trying to establish in the piece I'm writing.

Pam: It's funny. Since I subvocalize so much of my writing, and the sound of the words is so important to me, I've never been able to write with any kind of music playing. I can have ideas—and frequently do—when I'm driving or getting ready for work with the radio on. But writing? It would drive me nuts even to try.

What rituals do you use to get into the writing process?

Bill: I have two pre-writing rituals that I regularly use. The first is an exercise in freewriting. Freewriting is a technique in which you write spontaneously for a specified time, without delay or editing, any thoughts that come to your mind. The purpose is not to produce great work, but to prime the flow of words and shut off the internal critic that can so disrupt the process of original composition. I often do freewriting for five to ten minutes before I begin writing. The second technique is to brainstorm with pen and paper each section of the outline from which I am about to compose. This gives me the menu of ideas and examples I can select from as I proceed into the process of composition.

Pam: Another technique I've heard about is called "mind-mapping." It's making a two-dimensional visual flow-chart of the subject, its cause/effect relationships, and all its sub-topics. You can include pictures, arrows, whatever you want. It's great for people who have strong visual orientation. I haven't used this technique often enough; but when I have, the results have been wonderful.

You've told me that you do all your formal composing on the computer but that you used to do it by hand. Was this a difficult transition?

Bill: It was extremely difficult at first. I had written for years using Pentel Rolling Writer pens on reams of yellow legal pads. When I first sat at a keyboard, nothing would happen. It was like my brain was in my hand and no writing would appear without the motion of pen on paper. I was almost at the point of giving up when something clicked and I was able to finally make peace—if not an intensely ambivalent peace—with the computer. Today, I can't imagine writing without the benefits the computer has afforded me. Writing in the age of computers has brought untold technical aids to enhance a writer's productivity.

Pam: Do you feel as if you've lost anything in the writing process as a result of all this technology?

Bill: There are certain thoughts and feelings that, for me, require the synergy of hand, pen, and paper. It's like the physical connection of writing turns my thoughts and feelings to liquid that can flow out of me onto paper. I've sometimes felt like the ink flowing from the pen onto the paper in front of me was my own emotional blood leaving my body. I've never had that sensation striking keys and watching words appear on a computer screen. My journaling allows me to get certain things out of me through handwriting that may be harder to release to a machine. I know other writers who talk about this electrical fusion with their computers in which the machine extracts their inner work and the writer and the machine become one. I deeply appreciate what modern computers have done to enhance my productivity but I've never had any such mystical experiences with them.

Pam: Nor have I, but I seem to be kind of uncharacteristically utilitarian about the tools I use. For example, I love the computer for the freedom it gives me in composing and editing, but I have no interest in computers for their own sake. I have a difficult time writing without it, but I've never had a sense that it's an extension of me. Still, I've heard that some writers are very passionate about the tools they use: special types of pencils and pens, special kinds of paper, special dictating equipment, their pet word processing software, etc.

Bill: You get strange responses when you ask writers about these tools. I have a favorite story I once read on the subject. The playwrights Jerome Lawrence and Robert Lee, authors of such great works as *Inherit the Wind*, were once asked with what instruments they wrote. They responded that their best writing was done with a spade. You must dig into your subject and dig into yourself, they explained. You must always discover what is buried below the surface. I love this observation. Forget pencils, pens and computers. If you want to do great writing, use a shovel!

Pam: I won't touch that line!

Creating Time to Write

Pam: When do you have time to write?

Bill: You don't HAVE time to write; you have to create time to write. And then you have to fight to keep the world from stealing it.

Pam: Do you write every day?

Bill: I probably do some writing at least four days a week. The fact that I spend more than 100 days a year training and consulting means that much of this writing is done in short bursts. Whether during these periods of intense travel or blocks of time I take off the road specifically for writing, my writing productivity is quite variable.

Pam: Do you try to write at a particular time of day?

Bill: My writing schedule is dictated by my training schedule. When I'm training, my writing is confined to an hour or so each day and then several hours during the weekend. When I'm off the road, I generally write from four to six hours a day, every day. In my early years, I did most of my writing at night, but my writing hours have moved earlier in the day as I have aged.

Pam: That's interesting. When I have a day to write, I usually expect myself to put in eight hours at it. Then I feel guilty if I knock off after five or six hours. I feel better now that I've heard you say that four to six hours is normal for you.

I used to believe that I could only write well in the morning, and that my ability to think clearly would diminish as the day wore on—unless, of course, there was a deadline that forced me to write later. Now I realize that was more or less a procrastination device—an excuse to do something else in the afternoon

Sometimes I'm more productive in the morning, but sometimes the momentum of having worked on something for several hours will make it easier to write in the afternoon, or even late at night. The fewer restrictions I put on my writing schedule, the more I get done.

Inspiration in the Writing Process

Pam: Do you ever wonder about the source of the words you put on paper?

Bill: The words come from different places within me, and I experience their release differently. There are words that come from my head—it's like I can actually feel them leaving my mind. These words escape through a very cognitive and analytical process. These words are my words, but I feel some degree of detachment from them as if other writers could have come to the same conclusions and selected the same words. Then there are words and ideas that come from much lower and much deeper within my body. These words are words that feel like they could come only from me. These feel very personal and stir very deep emotion as I feel them leave me to enter the world.

Pam: What do you think of as the source of the words that come from deep inside you?

Bill: There is a very private place within each of us hidden from the outside world. The diversions of daily living and our fear of what we may find in this inner place mean that most of us visit this private retreat rarely, if at all. The writing self resides within this place. It is to this place of raw, unedited experience that the best writers visit again and again.

Pam: How easy or difficult is the writing process for you?

Bill: I've always been fascinated by, but have never understood, the mystery of the writing process for me. On my worst days, writing is like a difficult birthing process—mental contractions that go on forever without signs of progress. I sit staring at the keyboard waiting for inspiration, only to find the ideas and words held painfully suspended like false labor. On my best days, there are periods of such writing frenzy that, if you cut me open, I swear words would leak out. One must learn to tolerate such whims of the writing muses.

The sheer unpredictability and whimsy of this magic that brings the words defies everything rational. A day scheduled to write and the words abandon me; a moment between frantically paced meetings and the words explode as if driven by lightning. What is this force seemingly outside myself that brings the words? To whom do I owe thanks for the special pleasure that the words bring me? Writing can be hard and writing can be easy, but when it will be easy or when it will be hard is a complete mystery to me.

Pam: Do you believe in inspiration?

Bill: There are sometimes breakthroughs in perception of such overwhelming clarity that one is compelled as a writer to capture them on paper. The source of such breakthroughs has had thinkers and writers speculating for generations. The French writer Jean Cocteau often referred to being inhabited by a force or being who spoke through his writing. He said he didn't write, he listened. My best writing feels like that. It feels more like taking dictation than writing. There's a kind of spirituality often described by writers when they discuss the subject of inspiration.

Pam: Could you describe any personal examples of these types of experiences?

Bill: There are times in my training and my writing that I feel like the instrument of some mysterious power. I read words I've written, or listen to my words from a live recording of a training event, and genuinely wonder about the source of the words I'm seeing or hearing. There can be a depth in one's writing that transcends conscious understanding. In the heat of creation I've written some things in which it has taken me years to fully appreciate the levels of meaning contained in my words.

There is a heightened level of experience that happens to me during my best writing and training—I say "happens" because I don't have any control over it. It's a very potent and concentrated form of energy. What flows out of that zone sometimes leaves me spellbound. I neither own nor control this energy; I am only blessed by it. I'll write for hours in the hopes I'll experience the feeling of that energy for a few minutes.

Writing Productivity

Pam: Many writers worry about how long it takes them to write. How does one become a "prolific" writer?

Bill: I agree with the advice Janet Asimov once gave. She said to concentrate on GOOD writing and to "leave prolific for those souls who can't help it,"—like her husband Isaac, who wrote more than 350 books during his life. The only skill I know to increase writing production is mastery over the internal critic during the process of original composition. I think there's probably a natural speed at which each writer achieves his or her best writing quality. That's the point for which each of us needs to strive.

Pam: Is there an optimum production rate that you've come to expect when you're writing regularly?

Bill: My writing production varies from 500 to 3,000 words a day depending on the nature of the project I'm working on and the degree of physical and emotional energy I have available to drive the words. I think, though, that the trick in creating a substantial body of written work is not the speed of writing, but the consistency with which one pursues the activity of writing. It's more an issue of writing commitment than an issue of writing speed. I produce more than some other writers simply because I can and do commit more days and hours of my life to writing.

Finishing a Book

Pam: What special concerns do you consider when you're drafting the conclusion of a book or article?

Bill: Just as the introduction is your first opportunity to engage the reader's involvement, the conclusion is your opportunity to acknowledge the reader's participation and bid the reader farewell. The conclusion should close off the relationship with the reader in a way that fulfills the promises made at the beginning. I like to restate, often in a more provocative way, the thesis of the work and close with the personal ways in which the reader may utilize this thesis. I like to have the last sentences pose a provocative question, issue a call to action, or affirm the reader's importance in fulfilling the vision set forth in my writing. I want them to carry from my writing the core ideas and the experience of being recognized, challenged and uplifted.

Pam: Are there any danger points as you near completion of a book?

Bill: There's a danger that exhaustion and desire for respite can lead to finishing the book too quickly. This results in a precipitous abandonment of the reader. My anticipatory grief of letting one more literary child leave its artistic home can also speed writing during this period. And there's also the inevitable next project that has already begun to whet my appetite and fire my imagination. Sustaining one's patience and skills through this final end stage of a work is very difficult. It's the stage at which I'm most conscious of exercising discipline over my writing.

There is another experience that can happen as one nears the point of completion of a major work. I have experienced it with each of my major works and have heard other authors describe something similar. It's a sudden devaluation of that which one has worked so hard to birth. As authors approach the completion of a work, we move close to the time of our greatest vulnerability—the time when our work will be first judged. I think there's an anticipation of insult that provokes our own self-criticism and a desire, by discounting the work, to withhold it from public scrutiny. The impulse to kill it ourselves seeks to prevent the feared and anticipated injury. Who knows how many masterpieces never came to us as a result of such a process.

Pam: I wonder if the impulse is to withhold the book, or just to detach from it—grow a thicker skin where it's concerned. It reminds me of that phenomenon of parents and children getting on one another's nerves more and more as it gets closer to the time when the children will leave home. Just part of the natural separation process.

How about the process of getting the final draft ready for publication?

Bill: The most unpleasant part for me is the final revisions, approval of any editorial changes suggested by others, and the numbing reading of final proofs to ensure that no minor word changes have altered my intended message. By the time I finish this final stage, I'm usually sick of the book and have lost a good deal of perspective on how it will be received. I will later reclaim affection for the book, but at its point of publication I feel only exhaustion.

Pam: Do you feel an emotional letdown at that point?

Bill: While I'm writing the book, there is an acute sense that it is MY book. When the book comes off the presses, there's a feeling of detachment as if it no longer belongs to me—as if it now has a life of its own. There's a whirling mixture of satisfaction, relief and loss.

Pam: At that point do you feel like it's a stranger to you?

Bill: The book that has just become available to the reader is not fresh to me. I finished the book months earlier and am usually in the middle of new projects. For an author to talk about his or her "current" book is always old history because of the interminable time lag between completion of the writing and a book's subsequent release.

Pam: Could you describe one of your most difficult writing assignments?

Bill: Writers are always prone to think that their most difficult project is the one they are currently working on, but in my case, I believe that is true. I've just written a book that tells the story of the case management co-op of the AIDS Foundation of Chicago. In that book, I wrote a story extracted from interviews with the co-op founders, the case managers and their supervisors, and those people with AIDS and their caregivers served by the coop. They are as a whole a remarkable group of people for whom I've developed a deep respect and affection. I felt honored and yet humbled and intimidated to have been asked to write this story. It was difficult because the story is such an important one and it had to be told from so many perspectives to so many different audiences. It was also difficult because I had to remove myself from the writing—to inject my thoughts and my feelings would have been trespassing. It would have been injecting myself into a plot where I had no role. It was also difficult because their judgement of my work is so important to me. It was difficult because I wanted so much to write something that would honestly portray and honor their struggles and achievements—that would honor their lives. I've never had another writing project that has challenged and intimidated me in quite the same way.

Pam: Describe your feelings on the day you finish writing a book.

Bill: There is one brief moment in the creation of a book that is unlike any other. It's the span of time between the final proofs going to press and the book's release to the public. I try to savor this brief period of quiet satisfaction and relief at the book's completion. These are the last moments of personal ownership before the book is sent to its audience.

Pam: Have your feelings been the same at the completion of each of your books?

Bill: The feelings have been very similar. When I've finished a book and reflect over the process from the idea to the final editorial changes, there's sometimes a sentiment of disappointment that the work I created doesn't fully do honor to the vision that began the work. There are times when the work surpassed my vision, but this is less frequent. I think the author must make peace with each artistic creation and then let it go into the world to seek its own fate. Writing a book is like raising a child. At some point, you have to let it leave home even though you're not sure it's ready. You've got to let it go with all its inadequacies and still love it.

Pam: Have there been other critical stages in the completion of your books?

Bill: There's another stage that involves not my writing but a strange emotional phase I always go through as I pass the half to three-quarter mark in composing the first draft of each book. With all five books, I experienced an intense sense of my own mortality in the months preceding the completion of the book—an irrational fear that I might die before the book was finished. With each book, I left detailed outlines and editorial notes I thought would help someone else finish the book. As soon as the book was finished, this acute awareness and fear of death left me until the end stage of the next book. What can I tell you? Writers are weird!

Pam: No argument here!

Selecting Titles

Pam: How and when do you come up with the titles of your books and articles?

Bill: It varies. The title, *Incest in the Organizational Family*, was selected before the first word of the book was written. Final titles of my other books were selected close to their completion. A book's title can be very important, particularly when readers who don't know you are perusing thousands of titles in a bookstore. Lots of my readers are already familiar with the book content through exposure to my training, so titles may be a little less important for me than other writers.

Pam: Could you summarize our discussions about the title of this book?

Bill: There were several titles we considered. One of the titles I liked was *Dancing with Words*. Writers talk so much about the pain and agony of writing, I thought it would be great to choose a title that implied the playfulness and pleasure of writing. We settled on *The Call to Write* because it was more targeted to our intended audience—the aspiring writer. Our concern was that only those who already understood the role of playfulness in writing would understand the meaning of *Dancing with Words*.

Chapter 7

Readers, Reviewers, Collaborators and Employers

Sustaining the Reader's Interest

Pam: How do you sustain the reader's interest throughout the body of a work?

Bill: I think you have to provide readers with a range of stimulating and satisfying emotional experiences as they move through the pages of your creation. The sustained experience of a single emotion bores and exhausts. If I'm writing a piece that I want to arouse the reader's sense of outrage and passion to act, I must mix in softer emotional experiences to surround the central emotion of my work. There must be an ebb and flow through which the reader can move from intense emotional stimulation to quiet emotional refreshment. The reprieves allow an even higher level of emotional response than would be possible if there was only a single emotional theme.

Pam: That's sound advice, but I can't help comparing it with the techniques that terrorists are said to use when they've taken hostages—bring them to the edge, then calm them down, then bring them to the edge again. I know beyond the shadow of a doubt that you don't hold your readers hostage. But how does the writer guard against manipulating the reader's emotions?

Bill: There is a difference between manipulating a reader's emotions and being sensitive to readers' needs and interests. I try to be sensitive to the readers need for variety. I like to bury surprises throughout my work so that the reader is never quite sure what's around the next corner. Such surprises might include an oblique reference to some novel idea, a provocative question, the hint of a forthcoming revelation, the unusual word choice, a slight shift in style, an unexpected substory, an unusual metaphor, unexpected humor or some mild impropriety. The challenge is to inject variety without compromising directness.

Pam: How does directness engage the reader's attention?

Bill: It keeps the reader from getting lost. My general approach to non-fiction writing is: tell the reader the question you are addressing, your answer and how you will arrive at it. Then do just that. Go from beginning to end and eliminate every extraneous word, idea and story that doesn't enhance the pleasure of the journey between these two points.

Every written work is a self-contained relationship with the reader. The writer must introduce himself or herself, build the relationship with the reader, conduct the business of the relationship, and bring the relationship to a mutually satisfying conclusion. The directness rule is: don't waste the reader's time. When a writer wastes my time, I move on to other writers who treat me with more respect.

Pam: Do you try to promote particular political or clinical ideologies through your writing?

Bill: There is not a conscious attempt to proselytize as much as a desire to engage the reader in an exchange of ideas. I try to raise questions and provoke involvement in what I believe are important issues. I write my strongest statements not as the last word on a subject, but as an opening invitation for dialogue.

Pam: It seems to me that there's a danger at each end of the spectrum—one that the writer might be reduced to propagandist, and the other that the writer might explore all sides of an issue but never take the risk of declaring his or her own position.

Bill: Both of those states produce poor writing. I'm reminded of a line in a poem I once read by Louise Gluck. As I recall it, the line reads: "You know everything in the world but you don't believe anything." I think this captures the tendency of some writers to intellectually explore many sides of a question while failing to commit themselves to anything.

Intimacy Between Writer and Reader

Pam: How do you see the process of understanding that passes between a writer and a reader?

Bill: The best books contain open spaces—spaces that the reader fills in with his or her own experience. If the spaces are too small, the reader, like a bored voyeur, tires of peeking in on the most intimate musings of the author. The reader is cast in the passive role of an empty vessel receiving the words of the author. If the spaces are too big, the reader can project so much into the book that the writer's message is distorted and lost. I've had readers tell me some "most important point" they got from one of my books—a point that I know isn't there. Well it is there—in one of those open spaces—placed there not by me but by the reader. The work I write and the work experienced by the reader are always two very different realities. From this perspective, everything I've ever written is misunderstood—at least not understood as I experienced it. But that's what creates this magic between the writer and the reader. The writer's creativity is matched by the unique way each reader experiences and personally integrates the writer's words.

When just the right space is left open, the reader is drawn into the book and becomes a participant in shaping its meaning. The open spaces elicit the reader's own ideas and experiences. During these open spaces, the author gets to listen to the reader. Where such spaces exist, the reader becomes the co-author. In this sense, the best books are all collaborations.

Pam: I love that idea. And again, it all comes down to trusting the reader. You've said that the energy that accompanies the creative process can create a unique relationship between the writer and the reader. How would you characterize that relationship?

Bill: There is a complicity of intimacy between the writer and reader. Writing provides a medium for simultaneous self-disclosure and self-protection. I—the writer—can pour out my deepest feelings to you—the reader—and yet do so from the safety of my aloneness. You—the reader—may receive my deepest thoughts and explore your own responses in the safety of your solitude. Such connection can be remarkably intense. The beauty of a book is that we, author and reader, can achieve a unique type of intimacy while protecting ourselves through physical distance.

Pam: Is this how the reader gets to know the writer?

Bill: If you really want to know me, don't talk to me—read me! Like most writers, I've expressed myself with greater candor and clarity in my writing than I could ever do face-to-face. My use of the word intimacy to characterize the writer-reader relationship is deliberate. The popularity of books amid a declining literacy is not because people are seeking knowledge. Literary encounters between writer and reader are more about the search for intimacy than the search for knowledge.

Pam: Maybe one reason people feel particularly deprived of intimacy is that, as a culture, we've come to confuse intimacy with sexual activity—and almost treat the two words as if they're synonymous. Maybe readers are seeking from writers some of the elements of intimacy that can't be found in sex.

Bill: The encounter between author and reader between the covers of a book can be much more intimate and powerful than sex. Just compare the two activities. The literary encounter lasts longer, often involves more honesty and greater emotional involvement and it doesn't require that either party wear a protective covering.

Writing is such a paradoxical form of intimate communication. What other form of communication requires that you spend endless hours of endless days isolated from those to whom you wish to speak? Perhaps writing is a medium through which writers can work out their fear of intimacy from the safety of the writing desk.

Pam: Yes. And having an active function makes one much less vulnerable. In a sense, the person who's writing or speaking is really less vulnerable than the person who's reading or listening, because the writer or speaker controls the communication.

What do you see as the source of the intensity between writer and reader?

Bill: I think the source of this primitive connection is not about the writer's subject but about the feelings evoked within the words. It has something to do with the emotional architecture of human beings.   The memory of feeling outlives the memory of fact. It's the memory of feeling that the writer evokes in the reader, tapping that archetypal well of emotion we all share. The best writers evoke emotions from the days in which the chant, the story and the words of power were conveyed amidst drums and dancing and fire. They evoke the intoxicating pleasure of childhood discovery and the incomparable fears of monsters lurking within the darkness of our childhood rooms.

The Use of Readers and Reviewers

Pam: Do you use readers or reviewers while your work is in progress?

Bill: Very rarely. I don't want writing in progress contaminated by praise or criticism until my first vision of the work is close to complete. Praise of a partially completed work softens my drive and discipline, in the false belief that what I have completed is so good that I can coast through till the end. Criticisms of a partially completed work can puncture my ego, causing me to abandon the project to protect myself from further wounds. It's best for me to protect each work from the influence of praise and criticism until the initial composition is complete.   Once the first draft is complete, reviewers are invaluable.

Pam: At my stage of development, though, I need readers while I'm still working on that first draft—just to break the isolation of the process and give me a reality check. For example, in the manuals I've recently completed for PRC, I started with a sample sub-chapter, and got feedback before I proceeded with the rest. And even in *Worth Protecting*, Terry was out of town when I did much of the first draft. We'd had many long phone conversations about content, but that's not the same as getting a reaction to the written word. Finally I gave a chapter draft to some friends of mine, simply because I thought I'd go nuts if I didn't get some kind of outside confirmation that what I was doing was working. Fortunately, their responses were positive. It helped me sustain my energy while I waited for feedback from my co-author and principal advisor.

When you do finish the first draft, what role do your reviewers play?

Bill: I think every writer must find a small number of readers whom they can implicitly trust with each new creation. The purpose of such readers is not to provide unearned praise. Their purpose is to provide a critical appraisal of the work and to communicate their experience of the work in a way that the author can hear. I've been very fortunate to have had people whose combination of candor and gentleness has elevated the quality of my completed work.

Pam: It can also help the writer make up for being only one person with a limited perspective. I can send something out with a lot more confidence if I've incorporated the feedback of people with a wide variety of background and experience.

In the introductions to your books, you often encourage readers to write to you with their thoughts and criticisms of your work. Have many people answered this invitation?

Bill: A surprising number. The letters I've received have been helpful to me in many ways. The letters of appreciation for past works fuel my current writing. Letters sharing observations and posing questions force me to extend my ideas. Criticisms and suggestions help refine my design of future works. There are letters that warm me, letters that thrill me—particularly letters from other countries, and some letters that stun me.

Pam: What's an example of a letter that stunned you?

Bill: I wrote *The Culture of Addiction, The Culture of Recovery* for a professional audience. It's designed as a manual of clinical technique. Not one page was consciously written to be read by or to offer advice to recovering people. I was shocked to receive so many letters from recovering people telling me how helpful they found the book to their personal recoveries. *Culture* is an example of writing a book targeted for one specialized audience and hitting another completely by accident. That experience has forced me as a writer to think of secondary audiences in addition to the primary audiences I'm trying to reach.

The Benefits of Collaboration

Bill: Much of the writing you do is in collaboration with others. What's your experience of working with people in the writing craft? How does that element affect the writing dynamic?

Pam: Of course it has a very strong effect. I seem to have become so saturated with the collaborative principle lately that I have difficulty writing something unless I have input from others. It's that awareness of the limitations of my own perspective. I can feel in my gut when a writing process has grown too isolated, and I have to crack it open and let other people in. It's strange, because it runs so counter to my desire to control the whole process.

Bill: Does collaboration make writing easier for you?

Pam: It can make it much easier or much harder, depending on how it's structured and how good the communication is. The *Tools for Transformation* manual was my first experience of a collaborative process that made the writing much easier. We started it all off with a group process that got everybody involved in co-creating a very detailed outline. All the questions about what should and shouldn't be included were asked and answered in that session. What we came up with represented the collective experience of a number of people. The outline gave me incredible confidence in what I was about to write.

Bill: What setting did you choose when the writing itself took place?

Pam: The actual writing I did by myself. If I'm in a room full of people trying to word something right—or even with just one other person—it's ten times harder to think of the right words. I can think of concepts, and those actually can come more easily because there are other people's concepts to bounce them off of. But the final words are much harder to reach, because that "inner voice" either shuts up or gets drowned out by the conversation—or by what I think the others want to hear.

Bill: You mentioned earlier that the writing itself came more easily because you'd spent the time with the group pounding out an outline.

Pam: Yes. The writing felt like poetry coming out, very spontaneous. When you were speaking earlier you compared the birth of a written document to the birth of a child. I'd like to extend that metaphor to child development in general. If we give a child too much structure, the child doesn't feel any freedom or creativity; but with too little or inconsistent structure the child isn't safe: If she tests the limits she'll flop on her face. With the right amount of strong and consistent but flexible structure, the child is free—free from excessive limitation, and free from the dangers of having no limits. When I began writing from the structure we'd developed as a group, the process felt very free and very safe. Of course I made changes to the structure as I went along, but I could feel it around me the whole time, just close enough and just loose enough. I had the same experience last year with *Increase the Peace*—with *Worth Protecting*, too, but there's something about a group process that I've never experienced otherwise.

I've noticed an increasing trend toward co-authorship in *The Training Life*, too, and in some of your monographs. How have you structured those situations?

Bill: There is great variation in what co-authorship means and how the work of collaboration is structured. To me, co-authorship really implies co-ownership of the ideas presented in the work, not necessarily a shared balance in writing responsibilities. In some cases, one of the co-authors takes the bulk of research responsibilities while the other takes the bulk of the writing responsibilities. In other cases, all such activities are equally divided. What is most important is that there is extreme clarity regarding each contributor's roles and responsibilities within the project.

Collaboration Agreements

Pam: What kinds of issues should be clarified at the beginning of a collaborative project?

Bill: I'm still adding to this list as I build more experience in collaborative writing projects, but I think a beginning list would have to include the following

- What will be the respective responsibilities of each contributor?

- How will primary and secondary authorship be assigned?
- What time frames are expected to be met on the project?
- How will differing views about content or format be resolved?
- Will rights (and any royalties) for the work be equally shared?
- What are future expectations regarding use of the material?

Pam: Having been through a wide variety of collaborative efforts, I really appreciate those guidelines. Whenever there's more than one person involved in something, the level of complication rises. That has to be taken as a given in a collaborative situation. It can be planned for, but ultimately it just has to be accepted, and weighed against the enormous benefits. I don't know if I'm just getting better at avoiding the problems and complications that can come with collaboration, or I'm just choosing easier people to collaborate with. But in my past few collaborative projects, things have gone remarkably smoothly.

Bill: In your more difficult collaborative experiences, what seemed to be at the root of the difficulty?

Pam: One problem, as I've observed it, seems to be that we humans stumble around thinking that the world as we see, hear, remember, and interpret it is the One True World. Of course, we keep forgetting that others don't see, hear, remember, and interpret things the exact same way, so it doesn't always occur to us to be very clear and specific about what we think, want, need, and expect. We figure they'll "just know." Even the most articulate writers, thinkers, and group leaders can fail to articulate their expectations and questions clearly, and it can really derail the collaborative process.

Bill: Give some examples of this.

Pam: People can fail to communicate clearly about style, content, length, audience, goals—you name it! Everybody wants to come across as being very easy going and trusting, so we fall back on our presumption that what we want—or what we plan to do—is understood. Usually we don't compare notes effectively until a significant amount of work has been done and somebody's expectations have been disappointed. Then, along with the process of sorting out expectations—and redoing the work that has been done—comes the task of dealing with the frustration that's now entered the working relationship. In the past couple of years I've addressed that by trying to put all of my expectations into words, and making it easier for my collaborators to do the same.

Another problem I've noticed—in this field in particular—is that everybody's trying to do too much too quickly, and we sometimes make commitments we can't fulfill. Right after we promise to get our piece done by a certain date, the avalanche comes, and we're waist-deep in other projects whose deadlines are more urgent and less flexible. When one link in the chain is delayed, it throws off the timing of all the other links, and the schedules of many people are affected. All this takes place in spite of absolutely stellar intentions on everybody's part.

And then there's always the project where you're writing for a group of people who have wonderful but unrealistic ideas about what can be accomplished in a single document. Usually the idea will start out fairly simple and keep growing—the old "wouldn't it be nice if we could also include . . ." trick. Writing for a committee is especially dangerous, because each committee member has particular ideas about which bells and whistles are most important to include. And here we are in the human service field, where many of the people we want to serve are in painful or life-threatening circumstances. We'd feel like real heels saying "no" to any possibility. So in terms of its concepts, the idea just keeps getting bigger and more complicated; but to make it user friendly, we want to keep it short and simple and concise. The result is chaos.

Bill: How do you guard against these problems?

Pam: I really like your idea of writing out a collaboration agreement. I think I'd like to design a form that would include those elements, plus clear articulation of style, content, structure, limitations, timetables, contingencies, etc. Of course, these things have to remain somewhat flexible, because the information itself tends to change the project beyond people's perceptions and expectations. We might set out the most reasonable set of guidelines in the world, then learn a lot more and decide that the emphasis needs to change. Renegotiating the structure at that point doesn't mean we failed in our planning and agreement process. It means we're working on a different document, one that will be more useful to the field and reflect reality more clearly.

Control and Collaboration

Bill: Do you think there are any characteristics of this field in particular that make collaboration difficult?

Pam: Yes. I think there are some ways in which our people-helping instincts can get distorted, and these distortions are pretty well documented. I'm talking about things like people pleasing—my personal favorite—denial, the need for control, etc. Just because we understand this stuff—and teach others about it—doesn't mean we don't have to be very vigilant in our own work. And just because these tendencies crop up doesn't mean we've failed; it just means we're human. Again, that's what our contracts and agreements are for: to give us that structure that frees us to do our work.

Bill: How does the need for control interact with the collaborative process?

Pam: The need for control is probably an overriding problem for people in most fields, although our field's connection with addictive processes may give it a special intensity. And, of course, in collaboration we share control, and often have to compromise things that we thought were essential. But one of the things that makes effective collaboration so powerful is that we **do** learn to relinquish many aspects of control—or the illusion of control—and learn to trust. So not only is true collaboration particularly difficult in this field, but it's also particularly important for our growth as writers and as people.

Bill: What would you say to other writers who might have experienced some of the same obstacles you've experienced where collaboration is concerned?

Pam: At least I've progressed far enough to know that there's no magic formula for trusting people and letting go of my need to think I'm in control. I think most of the field is pretty sophisticated in this respect, too. People understand control and trust issues, and don't expect to fix them overnight. We've all faced down this demon a few times, and expect to face it again. I guess all I can offer is my conviction that the writing process mirrors so many other life processes, in that trust—often the most difficult thing—can be the most important thing. And complete control is impossible. I guess this is more evidence that our creative and professional needs can be in line with our needs as human beings. That gives me more confidence that we're on the right track.

Value Conflicts

Bill: Writing for a group or an organization can also present some challenges. Have you ever received a writing assignment that you strongly didn't believe in doing?

Pam: Boy, did I! When I was a reporter, there was a little boy in the community who was hit by a train and killed. It was Monday morning, and our weekly deadline was 5 p.m. that day. My managing editor wanted me to call the kid's family and interview them—ask them how they felt.

Bill: What did you do?

Pam: I told him "I know how they feel. They feel terrible, and they don't feel like talking to me!" But he was someone who didn't take well to opposition, and at the time I had practically no assertiveness skills. I was pretty scared of him. He also had his desk right behind mine.

I couldn't bring myself to call the boy's home, so I called my own apartment. I picked up the phone, dialed my number, and let it ring a long time. Then I hung up and told him there was no answer. He told me to try again later. Throughout the day I kept picking up the phone, dialing my own number, and slamming down the receiver, getting more visibly frustrated each time. Finally he told me to give up. I reluctantly agreed.

Bill: Have you ever decided to go ahead and write something you didn't feel comfortable writing?

Pam: Once, working for the same paper, I was assigned to interview a particular clergy member who worked in a local human service institution—sort of a human-interest feature. I thought, "Wow, this will be great! I can write about how spiritual and inspiring this person is!" The trouble was that when I met him, I couldn't perceive anything the slightest bit spiritual or inspiring about him. Everything he said seemed to be about the business aspect of what he did. Nothing in what he said—or the feeling I got from him—seemed to reflect any depth, sensitivity, sense of connectedness, or spiritual orientation. I also had this vague feeling that I couldn't trust him, although I still don't know why.

When I went to write the article, it was like pulling teeth. I couldn't write about how spiritual he was, because I hadn't seen any evidence of that, so I would have been making it up. I couldn't write something cynical, because that wasn't the purpose of the article. Besides, all I had to go on were my perceptions, which might have been inaccurate. So I finally decided to concentrate on the setting in which he worked, the people he served, and the practical matters he addressed in his work. It wasn't one of my better articles, but I got through it.

Bill: Have you ever refused to write documents because you weren't suited for them?

Pam: That's been a little harder—because I'd like to believe I can do anything—but I've learned to turn down assignments. First it's been a process of learning to tell which documents I'm badly suited to write, and which ones I just don't feel like doing. Then to refuse the ones that aren't right for me, I have to fight my people-pleasing tendencies. Usually I do this with the argument that, if I take the assignment, I'm really depriving the field of the high-quality document that would result if the right person researched and wrote it. Then I look to see if there's any kind of supporting role I should play—providing information, serving in an advisory capacity, or whatever—or if I should just stay out of it completely.

It feels really weird for me to turn down a writing project, but once I've done it, I feel good. I've proven to myself that I'm willing to defend my time, my skills, my integrity, and the quality of my work. Then the next time I begin a writing project, I do it with a little more confidence. I trust myself just a little bit more.

Editing the Works of Others

Bill: For several years it's been part of your job to edit documents that other people have written. How does that fit in with the writing role?

Pam: It actually provides a good balance. Editing is a very low-stress, low-risk activity for me. It also helps me with some of the lessons that collaboration teaches me.

Bill: Which lessons in particular?

Pam: Well, respect would be the most important one. I have to remember that, no matter how widely this person's style differs from mine, that's the style that he or she has chosen, and I don't have a right to change it arbitrarily, even if I think my style is "better."   An editor's job is usually just to remove the grammatical problems and clarify the points where the reader might get confused. If the people I'm editing want me to go farther, they need to tell me so in no uncertain terms.

Bill: Do you mean, if they want you to change the style of the work?

Pam: Yes. There have been a couple of manuals where I've gone through and completely rearranged the words to get a more casual and friendly style. But I've only done that after getting very specific permission from the person who wrote the original. I think any writer who's ever been over-edited knows that—if we haven't given that permission and somebody comes in and rewrites something we've written—it can be excruciating.

Bill: Has that ever happened to you?

Pam: Has it ever! I once submitted an article to a publication. It had a guest editor who was apparently very temperamental. I had a hard time getting through to her on the phone. When I did get through to her, her manner seemed designed to discourage further contact, so I didn't follow up aggressively enough after I'd given her my copy. When the publication came out, she had taken all the ideas and images, but changed the wording around quite arbitrarily, just to make it a couple of paragraphs shorter. The language had been very graceful when I'd submitted it, but she made it come out choppy and—in places—grammatically incorrect. Since then I've been careful to find out what people's editorial policies are before I submit anything.

Bill: Do you think that experience made you a better editor?

Pam: Oh, absolutely. I think of that whenever I take somebody's copy onto my desk. I talk to them first to determine just what kinds of changes they'd like me to suggest. If I'm going to mark my suggestions on their copy, I do it in green ink rather than red, because of the associations people have with red ink—teachers making big red "F"s and stuff. And when I bring people their copy, if I've made any suggestions, I explain the reasons behind the suggestions—either the grammatical rules or the ways in which the reader might otherwise get lost or confused—so that eventually they won't need me or anybody else to edit them. And I let people know that their decision to take or leave my suggestions is their decision.

Working With Others and Professional Growth

Bill: It sounds as if you've learned as much from the process of collaborating and working for other people as you have from the research and writing itself.

Pam: Yes. It can be sort of frustrating—especially when we begin to hit our stride as writers—to have to accommodate to other people's guidelines, take direction, make compromises, and follow their agendas instead of ours. But it's all valuable experience. There have been many times when I've been surprised to find that other people were right and I was wrong! The truth is that I'm a writer, not an authority. I still have a lot to learn. And things like taking direction and making compromises are valuable skills that I still have much to learn about.

Working with others also makes it necessary for me to decide which ideas are worth standing up for—and then stand up for them. Other people's opinions provide some resistance that I can work those muscles against. Just as working with people helps me learn to give in, it also helps me learn to draw the line and hold it. I need both of those skills to be a good writer, or a good person. I can't develop those skills in a vacuum. I need other people.

Chapter 8

Obstacles and Challenges

Pam: You've talked about the energy that can flow between writer and reader. Let's talk about what can block this energy. What are the major obstacles to writing?

Bill: Writers must regularly battle what Lisa Garrigues has called "the demons of procrastination, doubt, and distraction." I don't think anyone has ever said it better.

Pam: Are you easily distracted while writing?

Bill: There are only a few distractions that disrupt my writing. I usually try to restrict phone calls while I'm writing because calls inevitably pull my mind into projects other than the one on which I'm working. Other than that, I can write through about anything. I grew up in a small house filled with children. Learning to think in the midst of noise and chaos was a matter of personal survival. That capacity for detached concentration has greatly enhanced my writing productivity.

Pam: I don't envy you the noise and the chaos, but I envy the concentration. There were only two kids in my house and we were both pretty quiet. My sister developed a natural capacity to tune almost anybody and anything out—whether or not she wanted to—but I was the exact opposite. We're still the same way. Her powers of concentration are fantastic, and mine are—shall we say—easily interrupted. I might complain about it, except that it's the same permeability that, on a human level, allows me to perceive things that end up being valuable in my writing, or in interaction with others. Any tips on developing those skills in detached concentration this late in the game?

Bill: Some writers use particular types of music or sounds to block out distracting noises from the writing environment. For work on this book, I used tapes of Gregorian Chants that both set a mood of introspection and provided a kind of white noise that allowed a sustained focus on my subject.

Writer's Block

Pam: So, what's your experience with writer's block?

Bill: I think there is a lot of artistic posturing around the issue of writer's block. When my writing is blocked, it's usually one of two things. The first is a block of thinking. I can't write it because I haven't finished thinking—in short, I haven't figured out what it is I want to say. The birth of some ideas can't be forced. They require time for proper germination. That's not writing block, that's thinking block. When this occurs, you need to go to something else, the ideas haven't ripened enough. Franz Kafka's writing motto was one word: "Warte" (Wait). I think the meaning captured in this motto is similar to one of my own: "Flow, not force!" Waiting patiently in silence for the words to come is the meditative posture of the writer. When this posture is achieved, the words flow without need of inducement or extraction.

The second source of block to writing is physical or emotional exhaustion. The words may be inside you. There just isn't enough energy to get them out. You shouldn't be writing under such circumstances—you should be taking care of yourself. If I take care of myself and let ideas mature at their speed—not mine or someone else's—there is no such thing as writer's block.

Pam: I've certainly experienced both of these types of blocks—and I'm not above a little artistic posturing—but I still get lots of other blocks as well.

Bill: What are some of these?

Pam: Well, a couple of them I've touched on a little. Structural problems are the most common for me, and I've learned (the hard way) to look for these first. That's when my information base has expanded in directions I didn't foresee, and the structure I've devised no longer fits what I know about the subject. But I've usually developed some loyalty to the old structure, or the structure was the result of a collaborative process and I feel constrained to use it. Sometimes I don't see that it's a structural problem until I've been blocked for a while. Once I realize what it is, though, I just restructure it, and that usually eliminates the block.

That kind of ties in with another problem, the tendency to lose touch with my instincts about a subject. When I'm trying to do it all from my head, it gets much more difficult. Sometimes I get tangled up in my own brain cells. Or sometimes I'm trying to write the WHOLE THING at once, instead of just breaking it down into manageable parts and writing the one I'm on right now.

There's also the block that got me in the story about the clergy person I described a little while ago. If I think I'm expected to write something that I don't believe in, it drives me crazy. I freeze up.

Let's see; other blocks: Have you ever gotten stalled in the middle of a project? Yesterday you finished the easy chapter, and now you're trying to start the hard chapter, and nothing's happening? I read some good advice on that somewhere—and I've actually started following it. My tendency had always been to roll along through a chapter or section as long as it was easy, then break when I'd finished the easy part. Then I'd wonder why it was so hard to get started again.

But the trick is to schedule it so that you don't break after the easy chapter or section, but break in the middle of it—right where there's a lot of momentum. Much of that momentum will still be there when you pick it up, because your head has already been working on that thought sequence. Then when that chapter or section stops, start the next one right away, using what's left of that momentum. You're more in practice at that point. Don't break until you have enough of it done to store up momentum and confidence for the next session—and never break at a "stuck point."

Bill: I've heard that advice too. Does that help you?

Pam: Very much, when I can do it. We're trained to have such a mania for finishing things. We want to follow each thought through to its conclusion, thinking we'll be playing hooky or something if we stop in the middle. But doing it the way I've just described is much easier. There isn't that dread of going back and starting something new, not knowing whether or not I can write. There's more of a pleasant anticipation. I know I can do this chapter, and I was feeling good when I stopped, so I have every reason to look forward to picking it up again. It really helps me combat my tendency to procrastinate.

Procrastination

Bill: Ah, yes. How do you know when it's a real block, and how do you know when it's procrastination?

Pam: I found a wonderful book on procrastination that helped me a lot. It's called *The Now Habit*, by Neil Fiore. Its basic thesis is that procrastination doesn't come from laziness or lack of ambition. It comes from anxiety and excessive ambition.

According to Fiore, chronic procrastinators are something like workaholics. We usually tend to be perfectionists. We want to do too much, and we set impossibly high standards for ourselves. So of course there's a wide discrepancy between our impossible goals and what we know in our guts is possible. That sets up an incredible anxiety, sometimes on a conscious level and sometimes not. We start imposing all kinds of crazy restrictions on ourselves. "In order to do this right I'll have to work late every night this week, and all weekend too."

Now workaholics react to that anxiety by working too hard. They actually follow the crazy restrictions they've imposed! Procrastinators are smarter. We escape the anxiety. We daydream; we take a walk; we get interrupted; we do mindless paperwork. We tell ourselves we'll really buckle down over the weekend, but then we let somebody talk us into going to a Saturday matinee. In other words, we put it off. And the more we put it off the more anxiety and guilt we feel—and the more we need to escape. That's why so many procrastinators look like workaholics. Because when the deadline comes along we'll really put forth Herculean efforts to get it done. But that's only because we've backed ourselves into a corner.

Bill: So what's the remedy for procrastination? How do you avoid getting into that syndrome, or get out of it once you're in?

Pam: Fiore suggests a number of things, including replacing our counterproductive self-talk and actually scheduling adequate leisure time. You see, one of the reasons we procrastinate is that we've made all these promises—or threats—to work ridiculously hard. On some level we feel like we'll never again do anything just for fun or relaxation. We stop trusting ourselves to take care of that need. So something in us rebels, and goes and takes the time off anyway. Fiore says if we schedule ourselves not to work too long at a stretch—and also schedule fun things that we like to do—we'll actually end up getting more done, because we won't feel compelled to put it off.

Bill: Have you been able to follow that advice and get the results you want?

Pam: I intend to follow his advice, but I keep putting it off.

Seriously, though, I'm letting the concept sink in slowly. I first read the book a couple of years ago. It made a lot of sense, and it helped me break through the worst of the procrastination soon after I read it. Since then it's helped me become more and more aware of what I'm doing and why I'm doing it—or not doing it! Of course I haven't stopped procrastinating completely, but my patterns have improved a lot. It's to the point now where I sometimes start things long before they need to be finished, and finish them without having to stay up all night. That's really progress!

Loss of Confidence

Pam: And then we have those times when it's just hard to believe in ourselves and our abilities. That can freeze up the creative juices too.

Bill: Yes. This loss of confidence can come from many sources. Harsh or unjustified criticism can wound the writing self. The part of the writer that critically self-appraises can become aggressive and over-active. The harmony in our life out of which our creativity is nourished can be lost. Writing requires the ability to leap before looking, to let one's writing flow freely toward unknown destinations. If we are blocked emotionally or spiritually, we have to seek out experiences that will free the words. I've often recommended Julia Cameron's wonderful book *The Artist's Way* as a guidebook for those who feel their creative energy is being held captive by mysterious forces.

Writer's block can result from ego-consciousness. Creativity demands that we get beyond the self-consciousness (and the self) and focus on the product. When Julia Cameron talks about "our addiction to anxiety in lieu of action," she offers us a warning about how our own egos can get in the way of creative production. Physical and emotional discomfort must be shifted from the self into the energy of the creative process.

Pam: That makes perfect sense to me. The ego is so small, so limited, and so self-absorbed. It doesn't care about the larger aspects of what we're writing. It only cares about what others will think of us when we read it. I can't see it being anything but an obstacle.

Bill: So do you see any connections among all the different obstacles we've mentioned—any common themes?

Pam: Yes: Fear. When you think of it, all the blocks we've mentioned are functions of some kind of fear. I might be afraid of looking at the material in a new way, or of taking time off to take care of myself. I might be afraid of letting go of the old structure I've defined and replacing it with a new structure that fits my new information—or afraid of offending my collaborators who helped create the old structure. I might be afraid to trust my instincts, or just afraid of the magnitude and complexity of the project as a whole. Maybe I'm afraid to tackle a challenging part of the project, or afraid to start a new part. And maybe I'm afraid to challenge others' opinions of me, or afraid to put my ego aside and just write what needs to be written.

In procrastination, the fear can be overwhelming. It's fear of not doing it perfectly and completely, of not doing something spectacular. It's also fear that I'll never again get to rest and goof off, and fear of the isolation that can happen in the solitary phases of writing.

Bill: Do you find that locating and addressing the specific fear helps remove the block?

Pam: Definitely. Everybody's afraid, but the people who actually go ahead and do things tend to do so in spite of fear, not in its absence. The fear goes away only when we've been doing it for a while. I've run into that concept in a number of places, including a very useful book called *Feel the Fear and Do it Anyway*, by Susan Jeffers.

Bill: You're talking about "walking through the fear" in the writing process?

Pam: Yes. It does work. As you said, just write **something** for a while, even if you're not sure yet what you want to write. For me, the beauty of walking through the fear is like the beauty of walking through any other form of discomfort: That's where the best insights are. That's where we learn to write on deeper and higher levels.

Writers and Addictions

Pam: We've talked about the need for control, an over-active "internal critic," and internal emotional turmoil among writers. Do you see any relationship between those states and the tendency that a lot of famous writers have had toward alcoholism and addictive patterns in general?

Bill: There seems to be a growing interest in the American writer's vulnerability to alcoholism, prompted in part by new books such as Donald Goodwin's *Alcohol and the Writer* and Tom Dardis' book, *The Thirsty Muse*.

There are many things which could account for this connection between alcohol and the writer, but one of them must surely be the ability of the bottle to silence this internal critic we have discussed. Unfortunately, the creative fire is also extinguished in the process. Alcohol may render one free to speak, only to discover that, under its influence, one has nothing of value to say. If we look at America's great alcoholic writers—Lewis, Faulkner, Fitzgerald, Hemingway, Wolfe, Millay, London, Parker, Hammet, Williams, Cheever, Capote and many others, they produced their best work early in their careers. Writing, like everything else, deteriorates through the progression of alcoholism. Writers must be very careful, however, in linking their alcoholism to their writing craft.

Pam: What do you mean?

Bill: Alcoholism interacts with writing as it would with any professional endeavor. To attribute one's craft as the *cause* of one's alcoholism has not proved a helpful framework for recovery or sustained excellence in writing. William Seabrook, for example, wrote a fascinating book in 1936—*Asylum*—in which he attributed his alcoholism and psychiatric institutionalization to emotional blocks related to his writing process. The book ends with Seabrook's belief that these blocks were resolved. Seabrook later returned to drinking with the belief that his problems were now behind him. The progression of his alcoholism continued, ending with his suicide in 1945 at the age of 59.

Pam: What about writers' vulnerability to other drugs—which, of course, they've claimed as a stimulus to creativity?

Bill: As natural born risk-takers, writers are likely to always be on or beyond the boundary of the cultural rules governing drug consumption. There is a long list of writers who have claimed drugs as the source of their creative inspiration and an equally long list of preferred drugs: opium, hashish, marijuana, ether, LSD, and, most recently, Ecstacy. Like alcohol, these substances pose twin dilemmas. While they may help loosen the internal controls that restrict writing flow, they also impair one's ability to then execute one's craft with clarity, continuity, and power. While many writers have experimented with artificial stimulants to creativity, most conclude in retrospect that such experiments failed to produce a sustained body of valuable work.

Pam: Do you think it's some component in writers' natures that makes those experiments seem more attractive?

Bill: It's not that writing makes people drink; it's that the same emotional sensitivities that inspire great writing may also increase one's vulnerability for substance abuse as well as any number of other excesses of temperament or behavior.

Confronting Your Shadow

Pam: There's this stereotype that says writers are a little closer to insanity than other people.

Bill: Writers are drawn to unexplored areas of experience within themselves and others. The risks of self-shattering perceptions are always greater in this unknown territory. Tapping the pool of creative energy inside ourselves brings us very close to the psychic territory where the shadow resides. This is always dangerous territory.

Pam: Are you talking about the Jungian shadow?

Bill: Yes. Carl Jung described it as unacceptable parts of our experience and character that we have split off and hidden from ourselves—a process we do both individually and collectively. Writing can be a way to discover and make peace with one's shadow self. In writing, you have to be prepared to meet your shadow as you reach inside yourself—to discover unpleasant parts of yourself you have spent a lifetime projecting onto other people. By reaching deep within myself in the writing process, I often discover within my own soul that which I have most self-righteously hated in others.

Pam: I don't even have to write to discover that stuff. I just have to drive in rush hour, or spend 15 minutes in line at a store.

Bill: There are all kinds of excesses of temperament and behavior writers can develop in response to such painful self-confrontations. It can lead to craziness as well as healing and wholeness.

Pam: The predominant myth says that our creativity and our passion to write are driven by our pathology. But what I've experienced and observed tells me that much of our human pain is **not** productive of creativity. I think a lot of people notice those few who turn their pain into genius—and then think that they're seeing cause and effect. So they prod themselves into pain and self-destruction, thinking that's the one sure way to immortality. Most often it's not. Most often self-induced or self-aggravated pain is merely a self-indulgent smoke-screen.

But let's take the example of the writer who's legitimately confronted with his or her shadow? What response is most likely to enhance the health of the writer and potential readers—and use the energy from that confrontation in a creative way?

Bill: I think the writer begins by telling us the truth that the worst evil we have condemned in others lies hidden within ourselves. By exposing the shadow, it allows us to become whole. It reduces our need to kill parts of ourself we have projected onto those we fear and hate. By acknowledging the shadow, we bring it into some degree of conscious control. We inhibit its ability to shape how we perceive and act.

Pam: It seems that the line between emotional excess that can spur creativity and emotional excess that can impair is a very fine one.

Bill: I hadn't thought about this issue much until I ran across Kay Jamison's remarkable book, *Touched With Fire*, which explores the relationship between manic-depressive illness and the artistic temperament. I don't want to romanticize serious mental illness—there is nothing in psychosis or paralyzing depression that enhances artistic productivity. But all such disorders exist in degrees and there may be milder, subclinical deviations in mood or thought processes that can influence artistic sensibilities and productivity.

Pam: What would be an example of this?

Bill: I think I've been mildly hyperthymic most of my life. I think it's possible that mild alterations in mood and thought processes can bring blessings without the curses that come with the more severe varieties of these same conditions. In the case of sustained hyperthymia, who wouldn't want to experience abundant energy, minimal need for rest and sleep, an intensification of physical pleasure, an openness to adventure, an intense and expansive flow of ideas, gregariousness, powerful and colorful speech, enhanced creativity and productivity, elevated self-esteem and unrelenting optimism as one's normal emotional state? Every day people buy books, seek out gurus and use every manner of drugs to achieve just a glimmer of these experiences. And yet it's only a matter of degree before one's life could be devastated by an extension of the continuum within which these qualities reside. The blessings noted above are the joyous mild side of what can be a devastating illness that destroys lives through grandiose delusions, unrelenting anxiety, hallucinations, aggression, and every manner of excessive and compulsive behavior. It's the milder deviations of mood which I think have long played a role in fueling artistic achievement. It gives one pause to wonder. Is my passion to write the product of a carefully developed craft, some spiritually inspired compulsion or some quirk of neurochemistry? In my own case, it may very well be all of these.

Pam: Do you think writing might be a vehicle of self-healing—a means of keeping the "evil spirits" under control?

Bill: Artists of all kinds have talked about the healing power of writing, painting, sculpting, dancing, acting, and on and on through the other mediums of artistic expression. In the end, it doesn't make any difference whether one's artistic temperament and artistic productivity come out of or come in response to aberrations in biochemistry or traumatizing experience. What matters is how well one plays one's assets and liabilities. Every constraint is a potential launching pad. In the end, what is important to writers is to write, and to do so in ways that bring themselves and the world a glimmer of understanding and joy.

Difficult Writing Periods

Pam: Has there been any period in your writing career when writing was particularly difficult?

Bill: The period that comes immediately to mind occurred in the early months of 1988 when I shed a two-pack-a-day addiction to nicotine. Smoking had for years become so intertwined with my rituals of writing that I craved nicotine every time I sat down to write. Writing became a trigger for relapse. I had to stop writing until I got enough recovery time to re-integrate writing into my tobacco-free life. The release of the *Culture* book was slowed down six to nine months because of this. People kept saying, "When is the book going to be finished?" It was really embarrassing to acknowledge that my book on addiction would be finished when I could learn to write without drugs in my body.

Other than this experience, I don't think I have as much problem with the words stopping as a periodic feeling that my writing has lost its fire. Sometimes this is the writing and sometimes this is simply my emotional state—it gets hard to tell which it is sometimes.

Pam: How do you tell?

Bill: I like to read about other writers when I feel too isolated or disconnected from my writing self. Reading the thoughts of other writers helps remind me who and what I am and usually gets my writing back on center.

Pam: What's an example of this?

Bill: Some time ago, I went through several days of feeling that the writing I was doing was stale. Taking a break from writing, I pulled from my library the published diary that John Steinbeck kept while writing *The Grapes of Wrath*. In this diary, he wrote about his dullness, about being assailed by his own ignorance and inability and, as he neared its completion, self-described *The Grapes of Wrath* as a "run-of-the-mill book." Reading about Steinbeck's self-doubts about what was to be one of the great American novels helped me look at my own work more objectively and rebound from the normal disorientation that occurs when one has been in the writing self too long without coming into the world for refreshment and feedback.

Part III

The Writing Life

Chapter 9

The Writer Within the Culture

Writing as a Calling

Pam: To what extent do you see writing as a calling?

Bill: There was no voice from heaven that commanded me to pick up the pen, but there has been an increasing sense of obligation and duty that has propelled my writing. There has been a growing awareness that this activity is part of why I'm here. I had no such feeling in the early years of my career, but with age, I've come to sense that writing is an important part of my personal destiny. I think people must ask themselves, "To what shall I commit my time and gifts?" One of the most important gifts I've been blessed with is my ability to communicate through speech and writing. To what cause I commit these gifts is unquestionably one of the most important decisions of my life.

Pam: I agree. For me, for a long time it was quite a difficult decision, too, because there are so many areas of need in the world. And they're all—in my eyes, anyway—more or less equally important. I finally had to realize that my interest in a subject might be the closest thing to a clear calling that I might ever receive. If I let my efforts be directed by my interest, among other things, I'm probably coming pretty close to fulfilling at least part of my destiny.

In this culture we tend to have a stereotype of the writer as the "lone rebel" in sustained battle against society. Do you think this image works for writers who work within a professional discipline—particularly this one?

Bill: Your reference to this image as stereotype is very apt. This image has grown out of a Western literary tradition that has depicted the writer as the ultimate individualist. African and Latin American literary traditions, in contrast, see the writer and artist as a man or woman who holds deep ties to his or her community and culture and a duty to subordinate personal interests to the needs of the community. In this tradition, the writer acts on behalf of and for the benefit of his or her community. I think these latter traditions provide a more viable framework for understanding the role of a writer who commits himself or herself to use the writing craft in service to a professional field.

Pam: I think so too. Who are some authors who might illustrate those two traditions?

Bill: A writer who most people would agree fits the "mad genius" stereotype of the writer is William Burroughs, author of such novels as *Junkie* and *Naked Lunch*. Both in his life and in his literary works, he demonstrated extreme individualism and a sustained battle against the culture out of which he came. Chinua Achebe, the noted African writer, embodies the contrasting style: the writer whose task is to serve his community and whose personal ambitions have been tempered by generations of powerful cautionary tales on the dangers of personal excess. I believe Chinua Achebe, and not William Burroughs, is the model for writers who choose to commit their skills to the service of a professional field. This stance says that writers must draw their sustenance from the field and use their gifts in the service of the field.

Pam: So you don't see yourself as a loner.

Bill: I'm not a soloist. I'm part of a chorus of thinkers and writers. I seek to harmonize my ideas, writing with an awareness of others in the chorus and a sensitivity to what each of us can best contribute. One of the things that makes the isolation of writing tolerable is the knowledge that other kindred spirits are simultaneously pursuing this same muse for the same purpose. Although I write alone, I have a very real sense of participating in this collective effort. I think each of us has to find our own voice and then join the chorus that is singing our kind of music.

Pam: What special role do writers play in professional fields?

Bill: I think what writers can do for a field is tell the people's stories, validate their experience, celebrate their struggles and achievements, and honor the nobility of their suffering and sacrifices. Capturing this experience in writing is what being a witness for a professional field is all about.

Pam: How do you see the writer's role in his or her culture?

Bill: I think the most creative writers always scrape themselves across the grain of the culture in which they're nested. When the cultural focus is on the collective, the writer must celebrate the individual; when the cultural focus is on individual self-interests, the writer must call for affiliation and community; when pessimism and cynicism become fashionable, it is the writer whose words must sing a song of hope. The writer is the antidote to the excessive swings of the pendulum of change. We are part of the feedback system that helps the culture re-center itself following its cyclical appetite for excess.

Responding to "We-Theyism"

Pam: Where do you see the culture now? As a writer at this moment, what grain of the culture are you pushing against?

Bill: We are witnessing our own social disintegration. Our social institutions and the social relationships that bind us together are dissolving, leaving a vacuum—a lack of security and safety that opens the whole world up to exploitation by demagogues of all persuasions.

I think the major threat to our civilization at this moment is we-theyism: the emergence and proliferation of closed systems organized around "differentness" and exclusiveness. The most hideous episodes of human history have flowed inevitably from the conversion of differentness into qualities of superiority/inferiority, which then get transformed into every manner of oppression and bloodshed. Once we-theyism has destroyed the sense of connectedness and oneness between "us" and "them"—and once it has destroyed the very humanity of "them"—the most unspeakable acts can be executed and justified.

Pam: I agree, absolutely. That metaphor could describe the institution of slavery, the wars against Native People in the United States, the pogroms of Nazi

Germany, the horror of "ethnic cleansing" in Bosnia, and the rise in hate crimes worldwide.

Bill: Those are all examples of we-theyism. We-theyism also explains why some Africans actively participated in selling other Africans into slavery. Black-skinned people capturing and selling other Black-skinned people into slavery to Europeans could be justified because of the separateness produced by we-theyism. We-theyism also explains why Native People, who collectively exhibited such deep respect for all nature and their environment, could practice the ritual torture and killing of other Native People. There is clearly a story of European-initiated genocide against peoples of color in the United states. But there is also a story of how we-theyism within and between people of color has contributed to this genocide. When indigenous leaders compete rather than collaborate, we-theyism disempowers. When gangs go to war, we-theyism kills. When dealers are "us" and users are "them," we-theyism kills. We-theyism justifies genocide, and we-theyism begets cultural suicide.

The same we-theyism that externally threatens a disempowered group of people can spread infectiously, leading to the group's internal self-destruction. If we preach hatred of and separation from that which is outside the tribe, we inevitably get separation and fragmentation WITHIN the tribe. Xenophobes always end up going to war against themselves.

Pam: It only makes sense. We can aim destruction outward for just so long before some of it starts to bounce back at us.

You spoke earlier about the "war on drugs" and its disastrous effects. What part has we-theyism played in our national drug control policies?

Bill: This can be seen as a sustained framework for our current social policies. The day we define drug users as anything other than our own children, we have psychologically prepared ourself for their murder. Did anyone really think there would be a war on drugs with no bloodshed? Of course not. Then whose blood was to be shed? What people would live their lives behind bars? We created a mythology that rendered the drug user "the other" and "them." We won't move forward until we acknowledge the truth that the dope fiend of western mythology is our own child. There is no "them"; there is only us!

Pam: Do you see this tendency reflected in professional fields as well?

Bill: The same we-theyism has fueled the specialization and fragmentation of health and human services within the United States. The treatment field has become an isolated specialty practiced within isolated programs within isolated agencies. Substance abuse treatment is getting increasingly isolated from our sister disciplines, our communities and the realities of our clients' lives. Rather than provide a model of connection and collaboration, we are part of the social disintegration that in turn justifies our existence. We can't respond to we-theyism within the world if we can't overcome we-theyism within the field. The treatment side of the field has much to learn from the emerging models of collaboration practiced by our preventionists.

Pam: So how can the treatment field address this isolation?

Bill: We can begin by building relationship bridges outward from our own specialties. We need our prevention brethren to teach us something about the big picture. The emerging central task of prevention is the rebuilding of connective tissues—the re-creation of community. This is being done by linking people together who have a common interest in the health of individuals, families, neighborhoods and communities. This process requires a shift from isolation to collaboration, from competition to cooperation. The number of people who see themselves standing and struggling alone is increasing and the number of people who experience themselves as part of a community is decreasing. The task of prevention is to reverse this equation. Human health rests on a foundation of connectedness and reciprocity. *We can prevent nothing without the glue of community. We can't enhance the restoration of individual health in isolation from the restoration of community health.*

Pam: What roles can a writer play in responding to the trend toward we-theyism?

Bill: When the whole world is disintegrating into racial and ideological factions, it's the writer's job to tear down walls and build bridges. What the writer will be asked during such times is to generate the mythology to justify such madness and to fan the flames of emotional passion into frenzy. It is the writer's highest calling to resist this role and to call nationalist truths lies—to say that the legitimacy and health of one group can never be built upon the murderous extinction of another group.   As writers, we can create new mythologies that bring "us" and "them" together. We must create new stories that show how differentness and commonness, wholeness and separateness can coexist side by side.

It has been the writer's job in all ages to forge new stories proclaiming that you reap what you sow, that what goes around comes around, that the chickens always come home to roost, that he who lives by the sword dies by the sword. The writer must launch a counter-movement against ideologies that turn people into enemies. It's the writer's job to vividly portray the humanity of "them," and to say that "us" and "them" are ONE! Writing as the conscience of a culture, the writer can proclaim: When we rape them, we violate our-selves; when we kill them, we kill our own souls.

Pam: You say "the writer must" take these stands. For myself, I agree that I must. But do you mean that every writer must?

Bill: Writers sculpt a personalized image of *the writer* based on how they perceive the world and themselves. When I say, "The writer must...," I'm not talking about any universal rule; I'm sharing my own definition of myself as a person and a writer. I don't for a minute believe that all writers will or should conform to this definition. Writing is a conscienceless medium of transmission. It can transmit good or evil. I remember as a young man reading treatises that justified the horrors of Nazi Germany. It was the first time I encountered eloquence in the service of evil. It was very frightening. It is the individual writer that breathes values into the medium of writing. I do, however, think a growing number of people of conscience, including writers, will be called to this intensified vision of community-building.

"We-Theyism" Within the Individual

Pam: I don't know if we can counteract we-theyism—or even understand it—unless we begin by understanding it on an individual level. That we-theyism would be the notion that we are, first and foremost, separate from one another.

Bill: Do you mean a sense of spiritual disconnectedness?

Pam: Yes. I see we-theyism in its most extreme forms as an extension of that individual sense of separateness and fear. I also see it as a holographic phenomenon. I think that we-theyism on each level—global, national, community, family, individual—reflects that on all the other levels. And as we've learned so thoroughly in studying addiction, recovery, and general health promotion, if I want to effect positive change on my environment, the one place I have to start is within—my inner environment.

Now if my vision of the world is still distorted by my own sense of spiritual disconnection, then when I go to write about the we-theyism that surrounds me, my words won't heal—they'll attack, no matter what my conscious motivation might be. In order to be what you've called a "loving critic" I need to get very honest with myself about my own fear and judgmentalism.

Bill: Yes, but can't a writer use that process as an escape, an excuse not to address societal problems that are escalating out of control?

Pam: Yes. If I thought I had to resolve or eliminate all my inner we-theyism first, I'd never get anything done. But until I face it honestly as it is, and understand it, and even accept it as part of my task in being human, I won't be able to formulate an effective and healing response to the we-theyism around me.

The Writer as Healer

Bill: This culture needs healing, and I think writers have an important role to play in such healing. Their ability to interpret our individual and collective experience through story can provide a form of mass psychotherapy that is desperately needed.

Albert Schweitzer once observed that healers are at their best when they awaken the doctor that resides within each patient. I think that's what writers can do—call forth the powers of healing and hope that lie deep within each person and each community. Writers can offer an invitation so poignant in its presentation that it awakens those powers slumbering inside each of us. They can heal communities as well as individuals. They can string bridges of words and understanding across chasms of ignorance and hatred. The vision is a noble one; the execution requires great courage and skill.

Pam: Your description of healing sounds like a call for participation, and participation can be scary.

Bill: This world is as likely to die from detached disinterest as it is to die from hatred. There are more people who don't care than those who either love or hate. It is with this mass of wallflowers who fail to raise their voices to promote love or to quell hatred that lies our perilous future. Writers have importance to the extent they induce the wallflowers into the dance. I was a wallflower within my own professional field for years before people whose judgement I valued challenged me to get into the dance. It didn't matter that I didn't know all the steps. I had to start experiencing rather than just observing.

The Influence of Family and Cultural Background

Pam: How has your family and cultural background influenced your writing?

Bill: Writers create out of and struggle against the culture which produced them. My family tree bridges traditions of the south and the rural midwest Both sides share a tradition of organizing and transmitting experience through storytelling. This preference for oral narrative has had a strong influence on my writing and my public speaking.

The narrowness of my southern, rural, and White cultural roots sparked a need to move beyond the boundaries of my upbringing. Malcolm X once said that White was a state of mind, not a skin color. That was a riveting concept to me. I decided to dilute my whiteness by absorbing the richness of other cultures That movement outside of what is comfortable and known became an essential element within the process of my work and my writing.

Pam: African-American writers often talk about the importance of using their legacy and heritage in their writing. Are you suggesting that White writers do something different?

Bill: My (White) heritage excluded a whole range of experiences within its definition of reality. The history, the art, the science that I was given as "the world" is only part of the story. I can't escape that heritage but I can broaden it. White writers begin to lose their whiteness when they open themselves up to experience the missing pieces. White writers need to learn to live on the fringe of their whiteness.

Pam: Are you talking about "losing" your whiteness?

Bill: I once read an essay by Reginald McKnight in which he rejected his designation as a Black writer. He called himself a cultural mulatto. I think that's what I'm after—a kind of cultural miscegenation.

The goal is to be whole. If there is a metaphorical goal described in color, we should all strive to become black. I don't mean black skin or African-American culture. If white is the absence of all color and black is the presence of all colors, wholeness is the ability to experience all the colors.

Pam: I don't know. I think for many writers that will work as a goal, because they're at a point where they've chosen to accept and transcend some of their cultural limitations. But for many others, the cultural wounds and fears are just too deep. It may be all they can do to explore their own cultural terrain and work at acceptance and healing there. Or if they attempted to embrace other cultures and it might be completely false, and insulting to the people of those cultures. After all, we all still have the challenge of getting beyond our individual skin, too. Even to accept a few other people can be a lifetime's challenge, let alone the task of accepting one's own culture or the full spectrum of cultures.

Still, I love that vision of wholeness. How do you work toward it?

Bill: Any culture in which we are raised focuses our attention on certain aspects of experience and blocks our access to other experiences. The best writers have the ability to both step outside and see what is invisible within their own cultural experience and to reach out to other cultures to find new sources of knowledge and experience. Each book becomes a way to propel oneself inward toward one's own roots and propel oneself outward toward the cultural frontiers. The journey toward wholeness must always begin with a confrontation with one's deepest roots and proceed outward to the discovery of new dimensions of experience and character.

Pam: So you have to leave home to get home?

Bill: Yes. What I thought was reality was only roots—the blinders that filtered and defined what I saw and how I interpreted my world. What I thought was reality was only my immersion in a dominant culture. It was only by getting outside myself—seeing my maleness and my whiteness from the outside—that I began to redefine who I was.

Pam: But you had to start by accepting and understanding your maleness and whiteness. I've always been fascinated by cultures other than my own, but I think my ability to really celebrate them—and champion their value—didn't begin until I found a piece of my own heritage to embrace.

Bill: What form did that take?

Pam: My cultural background is largely Irish, with a few other countries scattered in there in smaller proportions. When I finally found the Celtic harp and began playing it and listening to old Irish and Scottish music, I felt as if something in me were being completed, some thread that had reached out from ancient times and gone right through me—and would be continued long beyond me. It was only then that I began to understand how sacred all cultures were.

I understand that my being female and White is a limitation, as any gender or color or cultural background might be. But I don't want to lose any of it. I simply want to accept that it is limited and use the rest of me—the part that transcends gender and culture and probably even species—to travel as freely as it can through the whole realm of experience. The more of the world I accept—and even identify with—the more room I have to move, and so the more comfortable I'll be.

Writing as an Anglo Man

Pam: Your comments suggest that you see writers who are women and/or people of color carrying a burden that White male writers don't carry.

Bill: I think that can be the case. I have no constituency to whom I am held accountable. Loyalty and fidelity to the service of White people or men is not a criterion by which my writing is judged, and yet analogous criteria are routinely used to critique the artistic creations of women and people of color. Obligation for the Anglo male writer is defined as fidelity to one's values and artistic vision. No broader affiliative obligation is defined and enforced in the way it is for women and people of color. Setting "women's literature" or "African-American literature" apart can ghettoize and patronize even when couched in the mantle of praise.

I think the reason that African American writers like Richard Wright and James Baldwin left America for Paris was to break out of the straightjacket of a literary racism that defined them ONLY as Black writers. To write within this definition would have restricted them to writing out of and about a restricted band of personal and cultural experience. One's "special" status as an artist can be a vehicle of disempowerment.

Pam: I agree.

Bill: My empowerment came as a gift to me from this culture. I have not had to be conscious of it or struggle to achieve it. I inherited this gift because I fell into a category of people that the culture valued and therefore protected and endowed. Whatever achievements or contributions I make are not a result of greater genius. It's not that I have more; it's that I've lost less. I've had less of me damaged and have had fewer diversionary battles and obstacles to divert my attention. Blocks to my achievement have been personal rather than cultural. I had no world conspire to deform my character by crushing my sense of self-value.

With consciousness of this status comes a debt to be repaid to those whose personal power was diminished rather than inflated—a debt that demands some effort to use one's influence to help level the playing field. It is the ultimate arrogance of the culturally empowered to claim self-ownership of their success, oblivious that their endowment was purchased at the expense of those they are inclined to criticize for lacking character and initiative.

Pam: It sounds as if you're suggesting that White male writers must almost "resocialize" themselves.

Bill: That's what I'm trying to do—resocialize myself. There's an interesting story that might be worth sharing here.

A couple of years ago, I gave a presentation to the Illinois Coalition Against Domestic Violence. One of the participants, Mary Grube, approached me and commented on the frequency with which I used the term "impact," connoting aggression and force, when I was really meaning effect. She noted that there seemed to be a growing body of language in our culture that normalized aggression and violence. I was struck by her observation. A few days later I was writing a research report in which I was attempting to describe a multi-agency service delivery model intervening with addicted women who delivered drug-exposed infants. The first thought that came to my mind to describe this model was, I'm ashamed to say, a "human service SWAT team." What do SWAT teams do, for God's sake? They assault! What an inappropriate metaphor, but a metaphor that came easily to me as a man raised in this culture. A more appropriate metaphor may have been the gatherings of women—and more recently, men—that occur at times of childbirth or illness. My socially conditioned metaphor implied aggression; the latter metaphor implies love and support. It takes great effort to cleanse oneself of such socialization.

If White men are to learn to write sensitively about women or about people of color, they must get beyond their socialized male ways of perceiving and thinking. The challenge for the majority writer is to develop a minority conscience. To recognize and transcend one's socialization is the ultimate act of self-creation.

Pam: Do you consciously experience your writing as a "man's writing?"

Bill: I'm usually not conscious of writing as a man until I cross boundaries that are intended to exclude me, such as writing about what are called "women's issues." I'm trying to become more aware of how my maleness influences my selection and treatment of subjects as a writer and my selection of words and images.

Pam: Do some writers—you, for example—write things with the conscious desire to help your readers through that kind of re-socialization and search for wholeness?

Bill: Writers create works that range from open invitations for self-exploration to propagandistic tracts defining what people should think, feel and do. I think my job as a non-fiction writer is to move beyond the transmission of information to the transmission of experience and meaning—to provoke people to see and get involved. Each of us has cultural cataracts that impair our vision of the world. Writers help peel away these cataracts. This is not always a service for which the reader is thankful. Many readers may discover in retrospect that their personal comfort was enhanced by their lack of clear vision.

Pam: Do you believe Anglo men can write about people of color or women's issues with respect, or are you suggesting that their treatment of these issues is bound to be exploitive?

Bill: On the contrary, the issue of substance abuse among women and people of color is so important, we should all be writing about it. The issue is how we write about it and whose needs and interests are served by this writing. If I write about these issues in ways that only bring more attention to me and more resources and opportunities to me, I've acted as a literary predator. If I write about these issues in ways that bring more attention and resources to bear on the problem, I've acted as a literary servant. The same principles would apply if I were a person of color. Black or brown skin is not a license to personally pirate the stories of one's own culture.

Pam: Is there anything within the addictions field that draws writers of all backgrounds together?

Bill: Writers in the addiction field are always struggling to create more powerful metaphors about self-emancipation. The image of breaking free is a very powerful one in our writing and it's not just about breaking free of alcohol or drugs. It's about breaking free from all of the things which have externally defined and deformed us. It's about breaking free of other's definitions of who and what we are, and its about breaking free from our own self-deceptions. For some of us, chemical dependency is a metaphor for the oppressiveness and addictiveness of these images.

Writing as a Woman

Bill: What's it like writing as a woman in the prevention field?

Pam: Well, I was thinking about that a little while ago, when you mentioned that women's written works are judged in terms of their loyalty and fidelity to the service of women. I guess that's something I've always taken for granted. I haven't thought of it as a burden, except at those times when my loyalty to my gender comes into conflict with one of my other loyalties as a human being.

Bill: Do you find yourself identified as—or identifying yourself as—a "female writer," rather than just a "writer"?

Pam: No. While I identify very strongly with my gender, that identity exists fairly independently of my writing identity—although the two merge with no trouble when that's appropriate. Does that make any sense? I tend not to think of myself as a woman first and everything else after that. While I identify more with women than with men, my primary identification is with the species in general.

I agree with you that as writers we shouldn't be confined to writing about issues specific to our genders and cultures. I'd never want to be restricted to just writing about "women's issues." I think all human issues are women's issues because women are human, and the topics that might be thought of as women's topics are relevant to everyone. There are stories that need to be told that run deeper in my gender, but if I tell them without a sensitivity to the experience outside my gender, then I'm just guilty of another kind of we-theyism.

Bill: How do you feel about tackling "men's issues"?

Pam: I'm quite comfortable with that. I have a great deal of compassion for men. Of course there are advantages to being an Anglo man in this culture, but men in general undergo a great deal of developmental deprivation—certainly in terms of emotional and intuitive development. And many men today experience a sense of powerlessness that can be just as problematic as the sense that many women experience. Being male might bring certain advantages, but it also brings a number of unrealistic expectations, and some emotional constrictions that would make it hard for anybody to stay sane.

Bill: Do you feel as if your writing is taken as seriously as it would be if you were a man?

Pam: I've wondered about that. I don't think as a society we've grown past the point where some people lend more credence to something simply because it was written by a man. I don't know. People in the prevention field certainly respect the writing of someone like Bonnie Benard, for example; but what she had to overcome to reach that stature, I don't know.

In a way, many of the things I write about—or the facets of them that I choose to emphasize—might be considered "feminine" by some. I like to look at underlying belief systems, thought processes, and emotions rather than just talk about behavior. That sort of "subterranean" approach is one that some people might attribute to the fact that I'm a woman. I tend to be very logical—even excessively logical—but people might see that I'm a woman and presume the opposite.

Maybe if a man were writing the same words they might think, "Oh, if he's a man and he still thinks this stuff is important, then it must really be important!" Maybe to people with that prejudice, what sounds "emotional" coming from a woman would sound "powerful" coming from a man. I don't know. I don't have any evidence of that, but it seems in line with the way people have traditionally been trained to evaluate things.

Bill: Have you experienced any of that as an obstacle in your writing process?

Pam: I don't think so. If people were to take my writing or my thinking less seriously because I'm a woman, then I hope I would take **them** less seriously. I might get annoyed—and certainly amused—if I heard about it, but I wouldn't have that strong, kind of gut-wrenching reaction that I might have if I'd grown up in a patriarchal family.

I think my greatest advantage in this respect is my parents. My mother has always been a very strong figure. She went to law school in the early '40s, in spite of a lot of people's disapproval. She worked as a lawyer while my sister and I were growing up—and worked in the home, so we had the example very much in front of us of a woman who was holding down a successful professional career. Of course, it helped that my father believed in her and supported her while she was getting her practice off the ground.

I've never felt that my gender precluded my being logical, strong, or successful. Don't get me wrong: I've got plenty of other insecurities, but most of them don't seem to be tied to the way my gender affects my work.

Bill: Do you think your gender affects your work?

Pam: Something related to it does; it affects it quite positively. I don't know if it's the gender itself, or the developmental and social factors that have affected me partly as a result, but something has prepared me quite well to do what I'm doing. I think—I know—my writing is better and stronger because of some of the elements in me that might be considered "feminine."

Bill: What are some of these elements?

Pam: Sensitivity, for one. The ability to empathize. The ability to recognize my emotions and give myself permission to feel them and express them. If I try to write about human beings without having access to those abilities, it'll be much harder, and I might not come up with anything effective. Maybe that's why all that talk about my being "too sensitive" was so confusing when I was a kid. It left me feeling ashamed of what has turned out to be one of my greatest strengths.

And maybe that's why learning about the difference between sensitivity and reactivity was so liberating. It gave me a way to separate the sensitivity from the internal drama. It allowed me to see the sensitivity as a strength again, so I could start learning to use it for good purposes.

Gentleness is another element: the desire not to inflict harm. I know the playground tradition says that boys get discouraged from being gentle and girls get encouraged to be gentle little ladies, but I don't think it's worked that way for a quite while. By the time I was growing up, gentle little girls were getting teased and picked on almost as much as gentle little boys. And at best, the boys got encouraged to be aggressive and the girls got encouraged to be passive-aggressive. That's not gentleness.

Now that I no longer feel ashamed of having a basically gentle nature I've learned—first of all, how difficult it is to follow that nature—but finally how powerful that nature really is when I let it make my decisions for me. I'm a long way away from being able to do that anywhere near consistently. I still have plenty of petty fears and angers. But I can see some exciting possibilities for my work if I do succeed in learning that skill.

And, of course, women much more than men—and much earlier—are encouraged to see ourselves in relation to others, rather than just as individuals. That skill is critical in our field, where so much has to be collaborative and cooperative. I've faced some struggles in accepting collaboration, but I've had those relationship skills—and a strong will to relate productively—that I could call on to get me through those struggles.

Bill: You mentioned that you consider yourself "excessively logical," and yet you've also talked about taking an intuitive approach to your work. How do you balance those two experiences?

Pam: I think being a woman helps in that too. I mentioned earlier that I've read that in women's brains there tends to be more communication—more signals firing off—between the left and right hemispheres than in men's brains. That probably means we can juggle those cognitive and emotional tasks more gracefully, and see more clearly the relationships among them.

The idea that we'd have better communication between the hemispheres makes perfect sense in light of our development and socialization, too. From early childhood we're expected and encouraged to manage complex social interactions that little boys are often taught to ignore, and to make sense of emotions that most boys are simply expected to pretend they don't have.

So while boys may get more encouragement and direct training in logic and critical thinking, they may have a much harder time learning to integrate those skills with their emotional lives. How can you integrate something you've disowned?

Bill: It's interesting, all that's being written these days about some fundamental differences between women and men. Twenty years ago, we were fighting to establish some semblance of equal treatment. Do you see the current focus on differences as threatening those pockets of freedom and fairness?

Pam: I don't know. It depends on how smart we are—both women and men. I think the differences are being explored now because women are finally secure enough in our little bit of hard-won territory to relax and start searching out the truth—whatever that might turn out to be. I think it'll turn out to be quite flattering to us. But we can blow it by ignoring the differences or saying they don't matter—or we can blow it by exaggerating them.

I'm kind of leery of theories that ascribe too many of the differences between the genders to genetics and biology. But socialization alone doesn't necessarily explain it all either. I like concepts that explain things not only in terms of biology and socialization, but also in terms of the difference in early developmental experiences. It makes more sense to me if all those factors are taken into account.

I think there are more similarities than differences between the genders. I also think the differences and similarities are layers on the same onion. But I firmly believe that the most important thing to remember is that we're all in this together. Women and men are here to help each other, not play blame games or one-up, one-down. The extent to which we forget that is the extent to which everybody loses.

The Ethics of Writing

Pam: Is there a particular area of the writing craft that you're currently working on—not a particular project, but a skill or perspective?

Bill: I've become interested in the ethics of writing—in particular, the values that are reflected in the writer's relationship with his or her subject. I've been thinking a great deal about the concept of individual authorship and the broader obligations the writer has to those whose story he or she is telling.

Pam: What got you thinking about that?

Bill: I've been reading African and Latin American writers and what I find in these works has been very provocative. In some non-Western cultures, oral traditions have been so powerful and so enduring that it's only recently that even the idea of individual authorship has been introduced. This raises an interesting question: when a cultural or professional field shifts from oral to written knowledge, who owns the stories?

A very innovative program that has a rich oral history is Project SAFE, a program in fifteen Illinois communities that has served addicted women and their children. I've been the evaluator on this project since 1986 and numerous reports and articles about this project bear my name. Project SAFE is not my story, though. It's the story of more than 3,000 addicted women struggling with the hopes and terror of personal transformation in the face of overwhelming obstacles. It's the story of the women and men who work in this project as outreach workers, child care workers, child protection workers, counselors, and supervisors. It's the stories of unseen grandmothers and other indigenous healers who are the primary care givers of the children of the addicted women treated in this project. There should be thousands of authors of this story, not one! I just describe all the points at which the individual stories intersect and fuse into a collective story. It's more portraiture or photography than writing. How do I as the scribe help all these people achieve ownership of this story. I say this not out of false modesty for my role documenting the history of this project, but out of a genuine respect for and tribute to the people who created this story with their lives.

Pam: That reminds me in a way of the charges of cultural theft that Native Americans have sometimes lodged against anthropologists.

Bill: That is precisely the point. When an Anglo writer (or Native American writer, for that matter) enhances his or her reputation and financial resources through writings about Native American culture without contributing anything to that culture, then the culture has been exploited rather than respected. You have to leave your subject in better shape than you found it.

I've been asking myself whether there are writing contexts in which the very concept of individual authorship constitutes cultural theft. I think there are such contexts, and I'm struggling right now to define their nature. I think a key element is the notion of reciprocity. If I study Hispanic youth in the Pilsen-Little Village community of Chicago, I must return something to Pilsen-Little Village for receiving the stories of this community's children. If there is no reciprocity in the relationship between writer and subject, I think we commit a form of literary strip mining in which we use people, communities or cultures for our own advantage and then abandon them.

I've added a new slogan to influence my writing. The slogan is "Honor the Source." As I approach a writing project, I'm trying to ask myself questions like the following: How can the people in this story be given credit for the authorship of their own lives and their own communities? How can I enrich this person, this community, this subject? How can I respect and honor the source?

Pam: You seem uncomfortable with the idea of the individual ownership of ideas.

Bill: I can't claim ownership of ideas. I provide a welcome mat and, if I'm blessed, they come visit me. I don't possess them. The best ones will visit many people other than myself. Most of them will outlive me.

Pam: In these interviews you've talked a great deal about values such as honesty, discretion, and respect. What other core values should guide a writer's approach to a subject?

Bill: I've been recently thinking a good deal about the value of loyalty. I think we recapitulate in our relationships *with* many disempowered communities the same cycles of attachment, abandonment and loss that are so prevalent *within* these communities. How many programs and workers have come and gone within some of these communities over the past decades? We must examine such projects with a long view of their effect on the community. We have to ask: Did we raise hopes falsely and contribute to the community's further disempowerment? We must ask: Did we ask the people of a community to exert effort, take risks, and emotionally invest, only to find themselves once again abandoned when money ran out for the latest of a long series of ill-conceived and inadequately funded efforts? It's no wonder that such communities begin to view "professional helpers" with distrust and hostility and view our agencies as profiting from, but failing to serve, the long-term interests of the community and its people.

Now what does this have to do with the writer? I think writers have to build relationships with a community if they are to help that community tell its stories. They must demonstrate sustained commitment. I think the value of loyalty demands that we not abandon, that we find ways to sustain a consistency of commitment and involvement over time. As a consultant who moves in and out of lots of organizations and communities, I am very sensitive to this issue and have started to experiment with ways to achieve continued connectedness to those I write for and about. I want to leave something of sustained value so that my work is not experienced as exploitation.

Pam: I believe there are also some stories that shouldn't be told—things that are too personal to the subject, and aren't anybody else's business.

Bill: I agree. I think the ethical command to tell the truth does not preclude the writer's use of discretion and judgement related to if and when to tell a particular story. I think ownership of one's own story is sacrosanct until the failure to reveal this story violates other more important values. For example, the corruption of values and illegal conduct at the highest levels of government (Watergate) outweigh the individual participant's rights to personal ownership of their stories. In contrast, I believe a celebrity's HIV status is his or her personal story; and that such an individual should have the right to choose if, when, and under what circumstances this story is communicated. I think professional writing within a service discipline must be held to a higher level of ethical accountability than is commonly exhibited in newspaper and pulp journalism. To write and publish people's personal stories without their permission is a violation—a form of predatory journalism that has no place within a service profession.

Chapter 10

Roles of Writers in the Field

Roles of Writers in the Field

Pam: Who writes in our field?

Bill: We all write. We write progress notes and memos and reports. Only a few of us have thought about writing as a type of service activity that could transcend the writing required to perform our daily job duties. And yet there is a growing need for this skill within the field.

Pam: What roles are there for writers within the field?

Bill: There are a growing number of writers finding niches within the field. They're writing state plans and research reports and journal articles and newsletters. There are some full-time writing roles and countless opportunities for full time practitioners to use professional writing as a means of broadening and enriching their other service activities.

Pam: What special challenges do writers face in the substance abuse field?

Bill: There are several things about the treatment field that pose challenges to the writer.

We are a field without a known history and with only a meager body of professional literature. To take up the writing mantle is to do battle against a strong anti-intellectual tradition that placed its highest value on action and its lowest value on thinking, as in the oft-heard admonition to clients: "Your best thinking got you here!" Professional thinkers, particularly those who write, have always been a little suspect within our field.

We are a field that has been driven more by ideology than by critical thinking. We have evolved a language that is laden more with cliches than with concepts. As a result, writers are always breaking no-talk rules and setting themselves up as potential scapegoats. Merely asking people to reflect on what they are doing may be construed as an attack if the writer is not careful in how he or she asks for such introspection.

Pam: To be fair, though, I think that in any field—or in any human interaction—one has to be careful in asking people to re-examine what they're doing. Still, the defense structure you're describing does sound a little like addictive thinking.

Bill: That's really true. We feel that conducting a fearless and searching self-inventory is good as long as it's someone else, such as a client, who is doing it.

Pam: How does the writer get through this defense structure?

Bill: The writer can criticize the field on a particular issue, but if the writer really wants his or her concerns addressed by the field, great care must be taken in how this critique is framed. Shame-based confrontations with readers activate this defense structure and blocks readers' experience of the writer's message. Engaging the self-esteem of the reader through a partnership approach is much more likely to be change-eliciting. "We" messages are always easier to absorb than "you" messages.

Pam: As a writer, for whom do you speak?

Bill: My first instinct is to declare that I speak only for myself, but I'm not sure that's completely true. James Baldwin once said his role was to be a witness—to write it all down. Some of my best writing is egoless. The books I write are so deeply rooted in the field—in my interactions with so many people—that I can't claim full ownership of them. I think my job is to help organize the experience of the field—to tell our collective story. In this sense I try to speak for all the people whose concerns I absorb through my daily interactions within the field.

I've seen so many elders of the field pass on, their stories lost forever because we haven't found a way to get their words on paper or even imbed them in our memories. There is so much that we are in danger of losing. I am currently writing a history of prevention and treatment in which I hope to be a witness for the field—to tell the tales of where we have been for new generations of workers who will come with no memories or knowledge of what people and events delivered the destiny of the field into their hands.

Pam: Does the writer have a role in creating heroes and heroines for the field?

Bill: I think a very important job of the writer is to tell stories that eulogize our living heroes and heroines. A friend of mine (Rob Furey) recently wrote a book called *The Joy of Kindness* in which he discussed our hesitancy to praise the living. He believes this hesitancy flows out of our fear that people will later disappoint us. I was so struck by this observation that I've resolved to add the slogan, "Eulogize the Living" to my writing creed. In an era struggling to find heroes and heroines, the writer can take risks by celebrating the achievements of living individuals and organizations.

Respecting Our History

Pam: You have a deep respect for history. It comes through in both your training and your writing.

Bill: I pay homage to history because I want to make sure my reader realizes that my challenge to some prevailing ideas does not come out of ignorance of the field's history and traditions, nor out of an adolescent need to challenge my elders. I try to demonstrate my knowledge and respect for where we have been in order to build my case that we must go beyond the present to write a new history that embraces and extends rather than destroys that which preceded it.

History is also a way to honor the elders of our field. It seems the men and women who build professional fields are always envied and discounted by the organizers and profiteers who follow them, but there is an intensification of this process of abandoning elders within our whole culture. The aggressive early retirements and reductions in force in many fields have pushed some of our most experienced workers out of action, and the oral history of many organizations has been lost with the exit of these workers. Perhaps my celebration of history is a desire to slow this trend.

Pam: You seem to really care about the people who came before us.

Bill: When Sir Isaac Newton was once lavished with praise, he responded with the oft-quoted words: "If I have seen farther, it is by standing on the shoulders of giants." I greatly admire both the humility and respect captured in those words. In so many professional domains, we are losing our awareness that such giants did and do exist. That's what a loss of history does.

Pam: You also seem drawn to cycles of history, and to the rediscovery of past knowledge that's been lost.

Bill: There is a line from an old spiritual often quoted in the speeches of civil rights leaders. The line reads: "Truth crushed to earth shall rise again." Writers are often the instigators of such resurrections. Part of our role is to serve as the memory of our fields and our cultures. Besides the nobility of such a role, the discovery of such hidden gems of wisdom are always a great delight.

Pam: Do you see any danger in glorifying the past?

Bill: Such glorification can be used to resist needed change, but the history of the addictions field is clearly not a nostalgic review of "the good old days." To document this history is to bear witness, in almost a religious sense, to how this culture has evolved in its response to its addicted citizens. A focus on history isn't a call to move backward. It's a recognition that great sacrifices and contributions brought the field to its current state of development.

Pam: I also think that often, when people take a reactionary stance, the "good old days" they want to get back to weren't really as they imagine them at all. For example, in treatment and recovery, there are folks who advocate a confrontive, take-it-or-leave-it approach to people with addictions—and justify it by saying it's the traditional 12-step approach. But it's not. The people who pioneered the 12-step approach to recovery did so with quite a bit of patience, compassion, and humor.

Bill: That's true.

Pam: Would you call yourself a critic of the field?

Bill: No, I wouldn't. To be a critic is to have objectivity that springs from informed detachment. I lack both objectivity and detachment. I have deep roots and affection for this field—I owe it a great debt of gratitude. The role of writers is to observe the field and seek to speak out to protect the field's long term interests. I think part of my role is to speak out from within on those areas which make the field externally vulnerable. If we could have had more voices speaking out on our excesses of the 1980s—aggressive marketing, inappropriate admissions, excessive lengths of stay, and so forth—we might not be having the integrity of our inpatient and residential models gutted by restrictive insurance coverage and aggressive managed care.

The Writer as Conscience

Pam: To what extent do writers serve as the consciences of the professional fields within which they work?

Bill: Most professional fields go through cycles of excess. Writers are part of the feedback system that helps each field periodically re-center itself. It has always been the job of the writer to puncture shared illusions and tell unknown or unspoken truths. This role is not without its hazards. We need to remember Chinua Achebe's warning that "principalities and powers do not tolerate those who interrupt the sleep of their consciences."

Pam: What do you want your readers to experience when they involve themselves in one of your books?

Bill: I want my writing to feed my reader. I want them to feel nourished, to put my book down and feel like they have experienced something of substance and personal relevance. I want them to feel that their commitment to service has been recognized and honored. I want my writing to help them rise above the environmental flack and "keep their eyes on the prize." For the time readers enter one of my books, I want them to get outside of the routine of what they do, to fully experience the meaning of what they do. That's what I hope my readers experience. Only they can tell you whether this goal is achieved.

Pam: How would you characterize the literature of the substance abuse field today?

Bill: Our literature is unique in one respect from other fields of health and human service.   Until recently, our professional literature and the literature written for recovering people and their families were one and the same.   Other than a smattering of research journals that rarely reach the mainstream practitioner, there is a marked absence of literature written for the front-line clinician.   Let me give you a comparison.   If you walked down Michigan Avenue in Chicago and went into one of my favorite places on earth—the Stuart Brent Bookstore—you would find rows and rows of shelves filled with the professional literature of psychiatry.   How many bookshelves could we fill with books written—not for the public, or for policy makers, or for our clientele—but specifically for the addiction therapist or the preventionist?

We have a long anti-intellectual tradition that poses a significant barrier to the emergence of a fully developed body of clinical literature in the field. Clinical knowledge continues to be transmitted more through oral history than through literature. I believe the professional maturation of the field is contingent upon the creation of this body of literature. Those of us who can write have a moral responsibility to both capture and extend this oral history into a body of literature than can be passed on to new generations of workers.

Pam: You once wrote a paper entitled, "On Our Moral Duty To Write and Teach."   Was this the essence of that paper?

Bill: The premise of the paper was that our failure to develop and retain our human resources was the Achilles heel of the whole field.   Staff turnover within professional fields of human service has reached such proportions that it threatens the integrity of our most critical service functions.   We can no longer rely on oral traditions to convey the foundations of our knowledge.   The paper was a call for those with some tenure in the field to begin or intensify their teaching and writing activities.

We need to create rich and pride-evoking traditions within the field that provide guidance to new generations of workers.   Our oral traditions must be extended to the written word.   Writing is how we extend human memory beyond the reach of a single life or a single generation.   Our tradition of self-help literature must be expanded to create a solid body of professional literature.   I will take us some time to do this well.   We need a whole new generation o teachers and writers willing to make a long-term commitment to develop their skills in this form of service to the field.

Issues in the Prevention Field

Bill: What do you think are the most important emerging issues in prevention that writers should be addressing?

Pam: Well, one issue that should continue to be addressed is whether we place our primary focus on risks or resiliences. The field has been moving toward a risk-based approach, with our programs and services targeted toward certain pre-defined risk factors. But focusing on risk factors—and identifying "at risk" people and communities—really does label people and give them momentum toward losing faith in themselves. On a national level we all know the range of things that can happen when people lose faith in themselves.

Many in the field are saying that our services should be approached instead from the standpoint of resiliences—strengths and resources that exist in the individual, and the family, and the community. I think no matter where writers stand on this issue, we need to reason it out and put our thoughts out there.

Bill: How do you think a resiliency-based approach would look different from a risk-based approach?

Pam: I think it would look very similar but feel quite different. I think it's quite possible to address all of the same risks—even with some of the same kinds of services—but focus the bulk of the attention on the resiliences that are the flip-sides of those risks. There would be a psychological benefit, both for the field and for the constituency. It's much easier to generate and sustain energy if we're focused on something positive that we believe can be achieved, rather than something negative that exists in overwhelming proportions.

The beauty of a resiliency or protective-factor approach is that it talks about the things that all people need in order to survive and develop in health and dignity. Some people get most of those things by virtue of being born in certain families and economic brackets. Others get fewer of those things, or get different combinations of things. Our job as a field is to identify the elements of healthy living that do exist in people and help them identify with those elements; provide the support and training that we can; and join with people in an effort to secure the basic necessities of a healthy and dignified life for everyone. Of course none of this is easy, but figuring out what's needed is fairly simple.

Bill: What do you think the field needs?

Pam: Well, the one that comes to mind immediately is something that I believe: That the prevention field needs to acknowledge and make a full-scale, collaborative move toward structuring its efforts around culturally inclusive spiritual principles.

Bill: Do you think the field's recent tendency toward a more holistic, wellness-centered focus will address some of this need?

Pam: Yes. I think if it's done carefully, and in culturally competent ways, it'll definitely help a lot. I'm also really excited about the progress that's being made in persuading the medical community to look at non-traditional methods of prevention and healing. But there's much more progress to be made. We need to do much more searching into the possible ways of blending "prevention" strictly defined with wellness promotion. The result could be quite powerful.

I think the one danger in the holistic approach is the same as in any other approach that acknowledges the spiritual. Once we get outside the parameters of what's acceptable to all cultures, we come to elements that are going to alienate some people. For example, we wouldn't want to start talking about "channelling" in our prevention activities any more than we'd want to start saying Rosaries in a group of mixed religions. We need an approach that blends the core principles of all traditions but filters out anything that would divide or exclude people.

The prevention field has already started tapping into the spiritual strengths in communities. I think before we go much further we need to take a careful unified look at how we want to go about this. How do we accurately reflect the balance and unity of mind, body, and spirit? How can we pull in the best of all cultures, emphasize their similarities and still respect their differences? How can we use the best of spiritual traditions without pushing away the people who need us? We need some kind of systematic, fully representative effort to study these kinds of questions as a field. Unfortunately, these kinds of efforts are hard to quantify, which makes funding difficult.

Bill: And what do you think the public at large needs to know about prevention?

Pam: I think it's the concept of prevention itself. We go about our business, working every day with our presumption that prevention is essential, when probably the bulk of the general public doesn't understand it or believe in it at all. Maybe some of them say they believe in it, but where does the money go? Where does the media attention go? Prevention is too slippery. People aren't grasping it because it has to do with the future, and the future doesn't exist yet. They want something they can see and hear and touch. So when they think of prevention, they limit the concept to concrete things like immunizations. They completely miss the community-based, holistic concepts that the prevention field—in Illinois, at least—has learned are necessary. The voting public wants short-term solutions.

If writers in this field can do anything really crucial, it will be to help make the very concept of prevention understandable to the general public. It will be to help people understand on a very visceral level that tiny little seeds of problems get bigger, and one person's problem will soon be many people's problem. That if there's a hole where the basic necessities of life haven't been supplied, something's going to fill that hole—and we don't get to decide what that "something" is. Someone who's been raised to believe that he or she has nothing of value to lose will make that decision.

If we think the incidence of things like substance abuse and HIV/AIDS and crime are bad now, we should see how bad they can get if we continue to undervalue prevention. It's our job to help people see, hear, and touch the future, even though it doesn't exist yet.

And as if that isn't hard enough, it's also our job to give people—including ourselves—hope. We have to present hope in the form of prevention, in the form of general efforts toward human well-being. Without that hope, all our warnings will do is leave people with more fear and scarcity consciousness, and we can already see what that's doing—to the economy, to our communities, to everybody. We have to gather evidence of what effective wellness promotion really means, and how it really works in human lives and communities. Then we have to present that evidence in a way that will grab people just as hard as the violence they see on TV every night.

Political Correctness

Pam: How do you respond to the issue of political correctness in your choice of language as a writer? It seems like this could be related to our discussion of we-theyism.

Bill: Do we dare get into this? Let me say from the outset that I believe this is a very important debate that is being increasingly trivialized at both public and professional levels. As a writer, I'm sensitive to the power of language to dominate and repress or to liberate. The generation of one's own language can be the first step in personal emancipation and self-creation. To be politically correct at one level simply means a willingness to respect people's right to name themselves and shape the language that most directly affects their lives. At this level, I do try to be politically correct as a writer. Having said this, I must comment on how the issue of political correctness is being used within this culture.

Superficial political correctness has become a substitute for substantive dialogue and relationships between the peoples of this culture. It is a superficiality that rapidly deteriorates into acrimony, further detachment, and isolation. How can dialogue occur in a climate of hypervigilance and paranoia? We're not relating to one another. We're waiting to pounce and denounce or to defend.

Pam: I agree.

Bill: We need to establish environments within which we can move through fear and posturing to trust and openness. We have to get through the cultural stories to get to the personal stories. We need a climate where hypersensitivities can be defused, where early mistakes with words are not grounds for the termination of dialogue. We need to stick together long enough to become transculturally fluent. I think we have to eat together and play together and talk about the minutiae of our lives before we can discuss issues of great import.

Writers can confront this superficiality, open up invitation for dialogue and demonstrate through there stories how such relationships can and do occur.

Chapter 11

The Writer as Human Being

The Writer as Reader

Pam: What books about writing have you run into that might be helpful to aspiring writers?

Bill: There are books on many facets of writing and publishing, but the books I've been most drawn to are those that describe the writing process of other authors. Writing is such an isolated activity that one is curiously drawn to other writers' descriptions of how they do it. It's a peculiar form of voyeurism—this desire to peek into the creative process of another person. It's a kind of reality testing and a way we can begin to define the nature of the almost magical process that brings the words. Some of my own favorite books on the writing process are Annie Dillard's *The Writing Life*, Virginia Woolf's *A Room of One's Own*, Janet Sternburg's two-volume set of *The Writer on Her Work* and Jeffrey Elliot's *Conversations with Maya Angelou*.

Pam: I've also gotten a lot from that little book you told me about—*Walking on Alligators*, by Susan Shanessey.

Bill: There are many people who have offered techniques and advice about writing, but I don't think anyone has done a more detailed and worthwhile job of this than Peter Elbow. I believe his latest book, *Writing with Power*, is quite simply the best book ever written on the process and techniques of non-fiction writing.

Pam: Is there a single text you could recommend that answers the practical questions of the writer's trade?

186 Part III The Writing Life

Bill: The *Beginning Writer's Answer Book* edited by Kirk Polking is one of the more concise and practical of such reference texts. It's filled with answers to hundreds of practical questions such as when you must get permission to quote from other writer's work or how to submit manuscripts.

Pam: What's the role of reading in developing the craft of writing?

Bill: The best writers, somewhere in their development, fall in love with words. I think the way you feed the writing self—that wonderful inner organism from which the words spring—is through reading the best and most varied literature you can find. I think we must feed the writing self experiences—the vicarious experiences that come from reading and the real experiences that flow out of the actions of our own daily lives.

One of the most important steps in learning to write is learning to read and to read selectively—to sort through millions of words of foolishness to discover the few words of beauty and wisdom. You can't write great literature if you haven't experienced great literature. It's important that one pay homage to the classic literature within the field. To accomplish this, one must have a voracious appetite for reading. I spend a considerable part of my life reading the historical and emerging literature within the field.   If one is going to communicate to the mainstream of the field, it's important to master the tone in which such communication occurs and the professional argot that signals one is speaking from within the family circle.   Learning to read critically is the foundation of writing clarity.

Pam: Reading novels and poetry also helps one's professional writing—makes it richer, more interesting, more alive. Have you always loved reading?

Bill: I have vivid memories from my childhood of reading books by flashlight under my bed covers so I wouldn't get in trouble for staying up too late. I'm half blind today from all those stolen hours of reading. I've always collected books and had a special attraction to libraries and bookstores. I hate the thought of death because of all the books I will have yet to read and all the books I'll miss that will be written after I'm gone.

Pam: Is there a special approach to reading that can enhance one's writing skills?

Bill: Up to a few months ago, I would have just said to read great literature. A recent reading of Mortimer Adler's *How to Read a Book*, however, has opened my eyes a great deal. Adler explores various approaches to actually dissecting and analyzing a book that has sharpened my own design in my writing projects. I would highly recommend the book to both serious readers and writers.

Pam: Can a writer ever read too much?

Bill: You can be so absorbed in the literature of your field that you lose yourself. In learning to write, you must write yourself through the stage of imitation—through the phase where what has come before sets artificial constraints on what and how you write.

The Writing Persona

Pam: We've talked about how you generally think of the role of the writer. How do you see yourself as a writer?

Bill: Writing is an activity I am drawn to; it's not my primary identity. I was not the person who grew up wanting to be a writer. It was a long time before I was comfortable saying, "I am a writer," and I still rarely say it, even though being a writer is very much a part of my identity today. I resist "I am . . ." statements because they can pigeonhole. I wouldn't want to be a writer if that's all I was.

There is a writing process and then there is a culture of writing—a society of writers, a literature of writing, gatherings of writers for reading and workshops. The writing process and the writing culture are two very different things—one highly introspective, the other highly social. Some writers get so caught up in the culture of writing that they lose touch with the inner source that brings the words. Some writers have little contact with the writing culture; others use the energy and ideas they derive from interactions in this culture to nurture their craft. I tend toward the former. I didn't pursue this craft so I could view myself as a member of some exclusive club. Writing is a way for me to act out values; I draw my identity from these values, not the medium I use to express them. For the person trained in journalism or the literary writer, I'm sure this is a very different experience. But I don't think the writing craft can be elevated to greater importance than the goal to which it is directed.

Pam: How did you begin to incorporate the identity of writer into your persona?

Bill: I think this identity must be internal rather than some superficial image that one projects to the outside world. Cultivating the pose of a writer as some romanticized affectation won't do anything to generate thought or fill a blank computer screen. Henry Miller said in *Plexus* that early in his career he was so in love with the idea of writing that he couldn't write. Some writers wear the image of writer like a psychological skin bearing a Gucci label. They're not in love with writing; they are in love with being a writer—a romantic illusion that promises to grant esteem. Writing is about getting beauty and meaning captured on paper; it's not about posturing at parties.

There are advantages to defining oneself as a writer. It can help one link oneself with the broader community and traditions of writers. Identifying oneself as part of a community of writers provides a source of connectedness and support that one can draw upon. My willingness to participate in these discussions stems, in part, from a desire to expand my connection to other writers.

Pam: Can we separate the person from the writing persona in our field?

Bill: This field is much too small for such separation. The writer's legitimacy springs from how he or she conducts his or her personal and professional life as much as from the quality of the words placed on paper. Writing is a kind of sponge that soaks up the juices of the writer's life. Writing will absorb whatever we bring to it. There must be congruence between the life lived and the words offered.

You build a relationship with the field based on your character, not your written words. You write out of this relationship. You have to establish a relationship within which you can make mistakes. You have to transcend the cautious superficiality of political correctness and move to the borders of our knowledge and sensitivities—borders in which one is bound to make mistake because one is in new territory. If I can build this relationship with the field any mistakes I make will be pardonable because they will be seen as errors of inexperience and not errors of the heart.

The Character of the Writer

Pam: What do you think is the relationship between the true character of the writer and his or her writing or writing persona?

Bill: This question is an area of great interest to me. Literary critics have always been interested in how a particular written work flows out of the writer's character. I'm interested in how the writer's image or persona and the writer's completed work shape the writer's character. I think imbedded within this discussion is the secret of self-creation.

The substance abuse field has for more than three decades preached the gospel of "act as if"—the idea that if one projects strength and competence, one begins to feel strong and confident, and then becomes strong and confident. I think we can create ourselves through this process. We can create a mask, wear the mask, and become the mask. Kurt Vonnegut once said, "We are what we pretend to be, so we must be careful what we pretend to be." Only humans, through the power of their imagination, can transcend their animal instincts by directing and participating in the creation of their own character. What this means to the writer is that in projecting that which we wish to be into our writing, we actually become that to which we aspire. To paraphrase Aldous Huxley, we create the mask and the mask molds us in its image. That's what being human is ultimately all about—this choice-making and self-making.

Pam: Could you give examples of this from your writing?

Bill: When I wrote about "stress carriers" and "high priests" and other forms of toxic leadership, I would forever alter the nature of my own leadership style within organizations. What I learned from writing that book and its sheer existence continues to shape my character today. Also, you can't write a book like *Critical Incidents* without coming away with ethical sensitivities you didn't possess before work on the book began, and the fact that the book is out there with my name on it holds me to a higher level of ethical accountability. In this sense, there is a process of self-construction that parallels my work on every book. The selection of subjects and the stories one explores can be a powerful form of self-sculpting. All the words I write exert an influence back upon me. You could have great games with this. Does the author write the book or does the book write the author? I think it's both. We write the writing and the writing writes us. In writing a book, the author creates a chrysalis out of which the book is born and the author is reborn.

Pam: So you're describing writing as a medium of self-exploration and self-creation, as well as a medium of communication.

Bill: The writer uses the power of words to peel away the layers of the self and layers of reality. I sometimes feel the layers of my mask peeling off as I write my way through my superficial posturing in search of something real. The masks that fall away in my writing surround me like snakeskin fossils of my former selves. Each mask must be shed before the next temporary self can have life. When I go into my writing room, I kill parts of myself and give birth to new parts. The writer's tools are instruments of death and resurrection; the writer is simultaneously murderer and midwife.

Pam: What lessons have you learned from other writers?

Bill: I identify with Maya Angelou a great deal, perhaps because her life, like my own, has so integrated the intensity of public performance and the solitude of professional writing. I also admire her work ethic and incredible writing productivity. She has taught me that what matters ultimately is not any creative process or artistic posturing, but the product. My goal, like hers, is to create a body of cumulative work that in both quality and volume generates influence. Maya also taught me that writing must flow out of a process of living—that what you write and how you live are inseparable.

Pam: How intriguing. How frightening, too! What does that mean to you as a human being?

Bill: It means that in spite of and in the midst of my imperfections, I will struggle each day to live out the aspirational values imbedding within my writing.

Fear of Failure

Pam: What's it like putting yourself and your ideas out there in print—with the knowledge that you and your ideas will continue to evolve?

Bill: I have at times held back ideas that I didn't feel were fully developed and that I knew might bring me some future embarrassment. The problem with this position is that the field loses out on ideas which can stimulate its continued evolution. If we waited for each idea to be perfectly polished, no idea would ever find its way to publication. The issue isn't to always be right. The issue is to participate in moving the struggle for knowledge forward.

To release a work with the full knowledge that your views on the subject will continue to change requires a confrontation with one's fear of embarrassment and failure. Most people go through evolutions in how they perceive and respond to issues of importance in their life. What makes writers unique is that their move from immaturity to maturity is so clearly documented in the permanent record of their writing.

Pam: I agree. The fear of being wrong is a major block to inspiration. Most us are trained that way as children: Either in gentle or not-so-gentle ways we're punished for being wrong. And now that we're adults, even though we know intellectually that we can't get anywhere without risking mistakes, most of us have still got this internalized teacher in our head with a big red pen, just waiting to give us an "F." We start second-guessing ourselves, and hesitating at the wrong times. We're like the horseback rider in the movie who pulls back on the reins just as he's about to go over the fence. The horse loses its ability to do what comes naturally, and crashes all over the place.

But, as you're saying, I think we have to be willing to risk being wrong. We do have to be willing to ask the questions even if we don't know the answers—even, as Rilke wrote, to love the questions themselves, however difficult they may be.

How do you handle your fear of failure?

Bill: First by acknowledging that failure is part of writing. If by failure you mean creating writing that doesn't get published, we all fail. No writer sees all of his or her work published—much of it doesn't deserve to be published. If by failure you mean errors in thinking or an expression of an opinion that we later change, we all fail. But these aren't failures. These are part of the feedback and learning process. It's important to take risks that may contribute to the long-term development of the field. Someone once said of Einstein that he contributed to the development of new knowledge even when he was wrong.

Maya Angelou has often said that you may experience many defeats, but that you must not be defeated. For the writer, defeat is to stop writing or to commit acts of self-betrayal in the writing process. Everything else is part of the process.

Pam: Do you think it takes a certain arrogance to be a writer?

Bill: A writer could be arrogant before he or she began writing or become arrogant in response to success as a writer, but I don't think arrogance has anything to do with the writing process. I think writers, like many kinds of artists, must have a willingness to risk making a fool out of themselves through the highly visible display of their work. For some writers, this risk comes from a quiet confidence. For others, it comes out of an intense need for recognition and social approval or is a way to do battle with internal demons that challenge one's worthiness. Still for others, this willingness to risk is an act of faith in some force that will bring the right words. At different times in my life, I've written from each of these conditions.

Humility is an essential ingredient for sustaining quality in one's work. Humility is a deep appreciation of one's limits. It is not a denial of one's talents or an abdication of one's responsibility to use those talents to benefit the world. False modesty can be a justification for escaping the weight of this responsibility. It benefits no one.

Courage

Pam: Has your writing required personal courage?

Bill: Courage? I've never though of courage as an element of my writing. The real courage is in those I write about.

Pam: There's a quality of boldness in much of your writing. You challenge your readers. You even challenge yourself. That certainly involves courage.

Bill: My challenge of the reader is part of the way I challenge myself. I try to create writing that elicits the best within the reader and within myself. I try to create writing that challenges the reader and myself to reach deeper, to reach higher, and to reach farther out. When my writing becomes most insistent and challenging, it usually flows out of a sense of having fallen short of my own aspirational values.

The most influential people in my life have had the ability to challenge me without shaming me. That's what I strive for in my relationship with my readers.

Pam: What kinds of writing require personal courage?

Bill: There are many kinds of courage that can emerge through the writing process. There is the courage of self-revelation. There is the courage to break silence and confront no-talk issues within the field. There is the courage to take a stand on an issue when silence would ensure greater professional comfort and safety. The great writers all wander up to the opening of the dark cave and do battle with the voices that say, "Stay in the light. If you venture in here, we'll kill you!"

Pam: What's an example of this kind of battle?

Bill: For more than a decade, I've explored a multiple pathway model of addiction and recovery. It's based on the belief that we have greatly over-extended the boundaries of our technology and applied that technology to problems and populations of people for whom it won't help and could potentially harm. The model suggests the existence of multiple etiological pathways for substance abuse, diverse clinical subpopulations, and the need for equally diverse approaches to treatment and structures of long-term recovery. It has taken some courage to confront our single-pathway dogma, but this critique is a kind of loving criticism of the field. It's an enticement to move forward and a warning of potential backlash. The 12 steps cannot solve all the problems of the world, and when we speak as if they can, we risk the danger of a backlash that challenges our ideological arrogance and our scientific integrity. Challenging the field in order to protect the future of the field is clearly one of the writer's functions.

Pam: I don't think the 12-step tradition holds that those programs have a monopoly on recovery, or that the steps work for everybody. Bill Wilson even wrote the opposite of that in one of his published letters. There's a phase of belief in an idea—any sort of idea—in which the believer feels it necessary to make everybody else believe the same thing, as if somehow that would make the belief more certain. I think sometimes people get stuck in that phase, certainly in the world of religion. And I see that tendency at work, both in the more extreme wings of the 12-step-based treatment community and in the many people who blindly attack that community.

Maybe if writers want to help the field heal this split, we need to begin by helping people progress beyond this stuck point in their own belief systems. Perhaps if people were more secure in what they were doing they'd be able to leave one another alone and just do what they do well.

Of course, that takes courage too.

Truth Telling

Pam: You've often talked about the writer's responsibility for "truth telling." Could you define what you mean by that?

Bill: Telling the truth means more than keeping deliberate falsehoods out of one's writings. It means telling what has been, what is and what could be with great boldness, depth and clarity. Truth telling is getting the words of the writing self filtered through the writer's ego without contamination by pretentiousness or self-doubt. Truth telling is the ability to cut to the quick—to drive home the simplicity that can guide us through complexity. That's what the writer is striving to achieve.

Sometimes the story is the truth. Sometimes the story is a mask that covers a deeper truth. Truth must be peeled like an onion: layers of truths, truths within truths. It takes a lifetime to open all the layers to expose the core and with any luck we find ourselves.

Pam: You often use the metaphor of the mask when you talk about this.

Bill: I have always been captivated by masks. The mask is such a provocative metaphor of the contradictions between our inner and outer selves.

We each wear a personal mask; every day is Halloween. We each play trick-or-treat in our interactions with the world. When we peel off the mask we have used to deceive others, we discover underneath yet another mask that we have used to deceive ourselves. I think each of us struggles to find moments in which we can break through these layers so that we can encounter ourselves and the world in an experience of authentic and naked truth.

Writers use writing to peel away our personal and collective masks. Many writers are drawn to writing as a ritual of truth-experiencing and truth telling. I can get closer to naming and disclosing my own personal truths through the act of writing than through any other single activity. It's through that process that I see myself and the world most clearly.

Pam: How do you get to the truth through the writing process?

Bill: You have to penetrate and transcend your own myth. All writers are plagued by self-delusion. That's because the words have to pass through the ego to arrive on paper. The job of the writer is to write through all the self-created lies until the truth emerges by accident.

Pam: What truths do writers need to know about ourselves?

Bill: Just that. We need to know ourselves. We need to know the hidden corners. We need to know what we love and hate—particularly what we hate. I think we are always in danger of becoming a caricature of what we hate. Einstein once said that fate punished him for his contempt of authority by making him an authority. That's the kind of paradox the writer needs to understand and communicate.

Pam: Aren't there many truths?

Bill: Yes, the burning question for the writer is always: which piece of the truth do I tell?

Pam: Are there pressures that prevent writers from telling some truths?

Bill: There are extreme examples of such pressures. As a writer, I try to remember the existence of other writers who were tortured or put to death for what they wrote. I can't forget today that there are writers who awoke this morning under threat of a death sentence for words they wrote on paper. Writers in professional fields are likely to experience pressures far more subtle.

There are many forces that can silence. The most primitive forms of censorship wear many guises. Straitjackets can come with the most expensive tailoring. Shackles can come in gold as well as steel. An office can become a cell. Censorship is more than banning and burning. Censorship is making the personal costs of telling the truth so great that there are no products eligible for banning or burning. Do writers experience such pressure in a culture that lauds its freedom of the press? Of course they do! Silence is the sound of words choked to death as the price of one's survival and comfort.

Discipline

Pam: What about the writer's need for discipline?

Bill: I'll take discipline over raw talent any day. The discipline and fortitude to just keep writing may have more to do with one's eventual contribution than native talent. The trick to writing is to get back every day and put words on the paper. Many aspiring writers can, like myself, make up for lack of natural skills with a sustained commitment to work hard on improving the quality of their writing. The trick to my writing production is that I write during the hours more talented people are lost in procrastination. Nothing—not even uncommon talent—can compensate for sustained discipline.

What I myself describe in spiritual terms—those explosive peak writing performances—are in reality the logical consequences of an unrelenting work ethic. That mystical flow of words is not possible for one unwilling to invest the hours of preparation and priming. Art transcends technique only where technique exists as a foundation. Technique is achieved and refined through discipline and endurance.

Pam: Is there a particular work you think of when you think of the role of discipline in your writing?

Bill: I think of the books. I've never done anything in my life that required as much sustained discipline as writing a book. It's as much about guts and stamina as it is about skill and artistic craft. I often think of writing books as a kind of literary marathon—a game of physical and mental stamina.

Pam: How do you keep score?

Bill: You count the number of days you have the courage to face a blank computer screen. You keep score every day by counting the words you created and subtracting the unnecessary words and wrong words. What's left is your score for the day.

Pam: On the continuum between escapism and activism, where does writing fit?

Bill: It can be at either end or any point along the continuum. It depends on what you're writing and how writing fits into the total fabric of your life.

Activism has been a consistent thread running through most of my life, and I see writing as a way of participating in the struggle for personal and social change. Witnessing as a writer during times of great conflict is the way the writer does battle. There may be times when the writer must turn off the computer or set down the pen, and fully enter the world—to replace words with more direct action. There are times when issues cry out with such intensity that witnessing must be done with one's whole body rather than with just one's words.

I can't think of any person who illustrates this more than did Gandhi. Here is a person who influenced the course of human history—who is known as a man of action—and yet his written works fill some ninety volumes. Gandhi was a thinker-writer turned activist.

Writing can be a means of confrontation. Writing can also be an escape from such confrontations with the world or with oneself. Depending on what I'm writing and what I do with that writing, I can be using my craft as an escape from or confrontation with myself or the world.

Pam: How do you use it to escape?

Bill: I experience my writing room as one of the safest places on earth. When I sit down to write, nothing exists but me and the words. It's easy to dive into the writing process to escape whatever discomforts I may be experiencing outside my writing room.

Risk Taking

Pam: How important to the writing craft is the ability to take risks?

Bill: You can cut out your niche within the traditions of a family, neighborhood, community, or vocation and live a rich and meaningful life if these activities satisfy the call of your own heart. But there will always be others—the nomads and adventurers—who hear the call of adventure from beyond the compound. I think most writers are in this latter group, always pushing beyond the boundaries that seek to define and contain them.

Pam: What risks must the writer take?

Bill: You have to be willing to take risks with your subject and personal risks in your selection of writing projects.

Pam: What would be an example?

Bill: Taking risks with your subject is the ability to take a traditional subject and approach it in a manner that allows readers to experience it in a fresher and more meaningful way.

I think a writer can prepare a work whose primary goal is to break open an area so that others can surpass his or her achievement. To do that, you have to be willing to allow yourself to be used as a springboard. In many ways, that's how I approached the writing of *Critical Incidents*. I was confronted with two dilemmas. I felt that the field's failure to adequately address issues of ethical standards and ethical decision making constituted a threat to the very existence of the field. I didn't feel I was the person to write the definitive text on ethics for the field. My answer was to write a book that catalogued the range of ethical issues confronting workers within the field and stirred dialogue and debate on these issues. From this perspective, the book will be successful only if it sparks follow-up work by other authors—work that makes my book obsolete. A willingness to expose oneself to criticism as a means of spurring the field forward is one kind of personal risk-taking for the writer.

An example of risk-taking with format is the current "conversation series" of which this book is a part. Writing in this format is a form of risk-taking. I have no idea how I'll later look back and view this experiment. Will I see it as a successful breakthrough that opened up a whole new forum for expression? Or will I see it as an ineffectual gimmick?

Passion and Enthusiasm

Pam: I often find in your writing the same kind of enthusiasm you've become known for in your training. Do you find yourself consciously injecting enthusiasm, or is it just part of the process for you?

Bill: I don't think you can hold anything back. I try to write each paper and conduct each workshop as if it's the last thing on earth I'm going to do. It's like this discussion—I want to inject the best of what I have to offer. This could be the last time I ever discuss my thoughts about writing. It could be my last opportunity for service. You can't hold anything back for next time. No one is guaranteed a next time. Thoreau once wrote in his journal: "If thou art a writer, write as if thy time was short."

Each writer must find a source of passion and ardor—a burning fever to tell their story and to tell it in their special way.

Pam: Is this what you mean when you talk about power as an element of your best writing?

Bill: Yes. Julia Cameron calls this power *spiritual electricity* and Peter Elbow calls it *juice*—a combination of "magic potion, mother's milk, and electricity." Power in writing is eliciting words from the center of our experience and our beliefs. It's the ability to imbue our words with our breath and pulse beat. Power is the ability to touch the reader deeply—to forge a connection between the unconscious wells of energy shared by both writer and reader. Power is eliciting an emotional memory of the roots of our humanness.

Pam: You've repeatedly used the word "flow" to describe your writing process. How do you see the relationship between flow and power?

Bill: Flow is a term Mihaly Csikszentmihalyi coined to describe an intoxicating, timeless state of immersion in creative activity. Flow is what happens when distinctions between play and work dissipate into a pursuit of one's passions. Flow is what happens when the words inside me become liquid and gush like lava. Flow occurs when I shut off the internal and external critics and let my writing self take over. Flow is an infusion of power and energy. I try to honor and respect this power, not only for its intoxicating properties, but also from my recognition that this power is the source of both creation and destruction, of artistic genius and madness. I don't think it's a power that can be played with or manipulated without dire personal consequences. The closest the writer ever comes to truth is in this state of flow where all internal editing has ceased.   Some of this truth will need to be later edited for human consumption, as it's often too raw, too pungent, or too deafening in its original form.

Pam: You called this power a source of both creation and destruction.

Bill: I believe that the striving for personal significance—the desire to affect one's environment and to have that effect recognized—is one of the most basic of human drives. It is the power that drives and surrounds much creative activity. When this striving, this basic need for contribution and affirmation is crushed, acts of destruction can and often do rise in retaliation. Creation and destruction can both emerge out of this state of flow.

Pam: Can writers misjudge this power?

Bill: They can misjudge both the power that brings the words and the power in the words. The power in words is both real and illusory. It's important to know the difference. Describing a problem, even with unparalleled eloquence, is not the same as solving the problem. The intoxicating power of words can sometimes lead us to mistake delusion for truth, personal pleasure for social change. Writing the words can create the delusion of control and accomplishment. Writing a scene about making love is not making love.

Pam: You describe power and flow as if they are experiences that visit the writer on their own whim. Do you think a writer can do specific things to reach a "flow" state?

Bill: I can speak only for myself. I still can't consistently initiate or sustain flow, but I've noticed that such experiences have increased each year as the time I devote to writing has increased. It's like time is the sacrifice that must be paid before the gods give the gift of power.

Pam: Your description of flow sounds like a state of intoxication. Do you find the flow of writing becoming addictive?

Bill: I think it can. It can both intensify and block out experience. It involves a focusing of attention that obliterates consciousness of time. It blocks out one's day-to-day concerns. It can have both stimulant and narcotic effects. I think writing and reading could become compulsive rituals of escape. They can be active or passive, life-infusing or life-draining, depending on how they fit into the rest of your life.

Faith

Pam: Some authors mention faith as an essential ingredient of the writing process. To what degree does great writing require great faith?

Bill: Julia Cameron mentions in her book *The Artist's Way* that she has the admonition, "Leap and the net will appear," taped above her writing desk. This captures the essence of an experience I've had repeatedly: when you cast off the internal shackles and take that leap of faith into a creative adventure, the universe reaches out to protect and support you with what Joseph Campbell described as "a thousand unseen helping hands." I've always thought that what we call "luck" is some cosmic reward for such calculated leaps of faith. Writers have to trust themselves and have enough faith to leap into the creative process.

Character Flaws

Pam: How does the writer work around or through his or her own—I call them "unfinished places," but they might also be thought of as flaws or weaknesses of character?

Bill: I think you have to first know those weaknesses and then actively manage them. One of the mottoes I've used to shape my personal and professional life is "Rise Above." There are flaws of character and situational circumstances that can elicit the worst within me. Rise above is my personal call to suppress such flaws and detach from such circumstances. Rise above is the belief that there are values that transcend personal and institutional self-interest. Rise above is my admonition to detach from issues of power, politics, and personalities, to place the immediate issue within the context of enduring issues. Rise above is a strategy for self-possession. It says I have to seize myself before I can seize the day. I can be pulled into pushing my own arcane interests in the midst of partisan squabbles as much as anyone else. The worst within me can spoil the best of my potential contributions. Staying conscious of the need to "Rise above" helps rein in the pettiness of my own ego.

Rise above is also about the paradox of involvement and detachment. I think we have to struggle and yet remain detached from our struggling. It is this detachment, this rising above, viewing ourselves and the world with a third eye, that keeps us from waging war in the name of peace and other such absurdities.

Pam: That reminds me of the three kinds of tests or challenges that, in mythology, the heroes continually faced on their quests. In one form or another one of these tests had to do with desire, another with fear, and the third with convention. In a sense, all three pop up from time to time to distract me from doing my best work. I still have very little self-discipline, but I'm getting better and better at tricking myself into working. Until I get better at rising above, I'll take what I can get.

Sensitivity

Bill: You mentioned having been labeled "too sensitive" when you were a child. That label seems to have been attached to quite a few writers in their early years. Do you think it's accurate?

Pam: I have a problem with that word. I think in our culture we try to use the word "sensitivity" as a label for two very different things, one of them healthy and one distinctly unhealthy. We use it to refer to positive things like artistic sensibility—that ability to create and appreciate things that may be subtle but still evoke powerful emotion—and the ability and willingness to perceive others' nature and feelings. But then we use the same word as a label for those times when people take things too personally, or overreact emotionally. That's not sensitivity. If anything, it makes us less sensitive to others' true nature and feelings. A more accurate word for that might be "reactivity."

And what happens to people as they're growing up under this label? If they're lucky, they're praised for the kind of sensitivity that allows them to paint pictures and talk to wildflowers and actually notice and care about what others are feeling. Then the next time they react to something in an emotionally self-centered way, they're told they're "too sensitive." So two things happen. First, they start thinking that their reactivity is a function of the same sensitivity that makes life beautiful, so they develop a sort of loyalty to that reactivity.

Then they start feeling like there's something wrong with their basic nature. They know somehow that the genuine sensitivity is an essential part of their being, and here all these people are telling them it's wrong to be that way. When we tell a child "you're too sensitive," it sounds like we're saying "you shouldn't perceive what you perceive and feel what you feel." Now in human service fields we're finally finding ways of helping kids tell the difference between what they feel and what they do with it. But there are whole generations of people who were trained to confuse the two.

I think that might have something to do with why writers and other artistic types are so vulnerable to negative, self-defeating patterns. We simply never learned to separate our perceptions and emotions from our reactions to those perceptions and emotions, so we over-identify with the reactions. Somehow we think the negative stuff is part of what keeps the creativity alive, and the culture that surrounds us reinforces that myth—you know, the stereotype of the tortured writer starving in a garret.

Bill: So you don't think it's necessary to "suffer for art's sake"?

Pam: What's that old saying, "pain is mandatory"—at least if you're alive—"but suffering is optional"? I think that holds true even for writers. I think that negativity—the tendency to get caught up in our own drama—actually gets in the way of creativity. It distorts our perceptions and imagination, and blocks our ability to receive higher forms of inspiration. All we see is ourselves, and that's a small palette to paint from.

Absent-mindedness

Pam: We've explored a number of serious dimensions of the writer's character. One that people think of in a lighter vein—and one I've always used my writing to justify in myself—is absent-mindedness. If I only exhibited this quality when I was writing or planning something, that justification might be legitimate. But absent-mindedness seems to be one of the major organizing principles of my life. What do you think of that particular facet of the writer's image?

Bill: It's true for me. People who live with a writer must learn to be tolerant of those blank looks which reflect that the writer's mind has just left this world for a visit to a current or future project. Writers must be protected from themselves like young children or senile relatives when they are in such working states. Sharp objects, machinery with moving parts and sudden changes in elevation can all pose risks to working writers. If this quality of being scatterbrained was a crime, I would have no recourse but to plead guilty.

Chapter 12

Writing and Living Too

Personal Experiences and Privacy

Pam: To what extent are your own experiences incorporated into your writing?

Bill: Writers, including myself, are shameless about exploiting their own experience for their craft. Every shard of experience, every sharp-edged emotion, every emotional wound is turned into grist for the writing mill. The writing self is the consummate voyeur of its host; it's parasitic in its drive to create. There is a danger in such exploitation. You can reach a point in your writing zeal that you no longer experience events, you record them; you don't live life, you use it. For the obsessed writer, life is experienced secondhand, observed and recorded the first time through, fully experienced only when the words flow onto the paper. This exploitation is part of writers' proclivity for excessiveness. Writing should flow out of one's life experience, not **be** that life experience. Thoreau captured this sentiment when he wrote: "How vain it is to sit down and write when you have not stood up to live."

The craft that can absorb and discharge so much of the extreme in the writer's character can itself become an excessive behavior.

Pam: What about the issue of privacy for the writer?

Bill: Writers are people who violate their own privacy for a living. I would consider it a horrible invasion of privacy if another person disclosed information about me that I freely share to the world in my published work.

I think each writer has the right to dictate the limits of intimacy he or she is willing to offer in interactions with an audience. My general rule is that I'll attempt to respond to questions about myself that have a direct link to my work. Beyond that boundary, I tend to be very protective of my private life.

Pam: It seems that self-disclosure would eventually creep into any work, fiction or non-fiction. Doesn't this leave the writer very vulnerable.

Bill: The writer's dilemma is always how to tell the story while protecting the secrets of the self. The secrets move closer and closer to the surface through the act of writing and eventually enter the written work either literally or metaphorically. Perhaps that's one of the attractions to writing. Playing with words is like a Rorschach for writers—it's the way we safely exorcise our secrets and heal ourselves.

Fitting Writing Into Your Life

Pam: How do you fit writing into the rest of your life?

Bill: The trick is to create a whole life—to integrate the craft of writing into a broader life that gives pleasure and meaning. I think you have to work out a special synergy so that writing enriches the rest of your life and the rest of your life enriches your writing. The processes of my living and my writing are very intertwined today.

Pam: How do you get time for all the writing projects you get involved in?

Bill: As I get older, I'm becoming less interested in money and more interested in time. I spend time as if it were more valuable than money. It is! I fight off projects that are burdens, to make room for projects that excite me.

Pam: You spend more than half your time doing lectures and seminars. What's the relationship between your training activities and your writing activities?

Bill: The skills of training and writing don't automatically go together but there is a very close relationship between these two activities for me. Writing was my first love but I had to shift to training early in my career, when discovered that most of my primary audience didn't read. It was a great disillusionment to discover that my most important constituents would rather listen than read. Lecturing was a way of taking my writing on the road. If m readers wouldn't come to me, I would go to them. If my words couldn't reach my readers' eyes, then I would send my words to their ears. My training is an extension of my writing. What I try to do with my writing is to capture oral history and oral folklore of our field in print. It's like speaking on paper and the print is the tongue that makes the reader hear my voice.

Pam: Does your writing recharge you?

Bill: Writing is a wonderful way for me to pull back into myself—off the training stage—and explore new ideas. Through writing I can push myself into new territory that I would be terrified to venture into in front of an audience. The writer Ben Hecht once said that writers were frustrated actors who recited their lines in the hidden auditoriums of their own minds. I really think that is true. As much time as I spend in front of hundreds of people, I can still say things in print that I could never adequately express from the lectern. My best training performances flow from my mind onto a computer screen in the isolation and silence of my writing room.

I enjoy the solitude and privacy of writing as much as I enjoy the personal connectedness to others I experience in training. I find a wonderful synergy between my writing and training.

Pam: Which do you find more personally draining: writing or training?

Bill: I experience training as energizing. I usually feel I get as much energy as I've given. With writing, it's quite the opposite. When I'm bubbling over with energy, I am driven to write. Writing is an emptying of myself, rather than a replenishment. I walk away from the writing with a sense that something has been drained from me. Each writer must find a source of refreshment and rejuvenation to counter this emptying of oneself into the writing process.

Pam: That's interesting. I suspect that for me it's the opposite, but that may be because I feel more comfortable with my writing skills than with my training skills. The training skills have been developing for just a few years, while the writing skills have been with me most of my life.

What do you like best about writing?

208 Part III The Writing Life

Bill: So much of my life—my training life—is filled with the intensity of interaction. Training and consulting fill my life with a lot of noise. I like the quietness of writing. Much of the content of my training activities deals with the inner life of people; writing is a way to elucidate my own inner life. The content of my writing flows out of my living. The process of my writing flows out of my solitude. There is nothing I do that provides more intimacy with myself than the act of writing.

Success in Writing

Pam: You've talked about a lot of the personal rewards you've gotten from writing. Have you also gained materially from it?

Bill: I make enough money from my writing to support my addiction to acquiring and reading good books. It would be a spartan lifestyle if I had to sustain myself solely on income from my writing. Most writers will need some way other than their writing to support themselves, and this may be best. One can be so easily bribed and manipulated to use one's skills to create something for which one has no passion. If you're writing for money—need money from writing to support your existence—the danger of losing your personal voice and your personal vision is great.

Pam: Are there many people who make enough money from the sale of their books to make a living writing full time?

Bill: There are very few writers in any professional field who support themselves on commercial sales of their articles or books. Even those who may make a great deal of money on one or two books usually don't sustain their writing production and popularity to support themselves over the years solely from writing. Most of the people who write full time in the field are paid contractually to write and are not dependent for their livelihood on the sale of their written works.

Pam: So I take it you wouldn't recommend writing in the field as a way to "make a lot of money."

Bill: I can't think of a worse reason to write or a more inefficient way to make money.

Pam: How do you measure success as a writer?

Bill: Success is first and foremost getting time to write—having a lifestyle that accommodates your writing rituals, finding a way to keep the bills paid so you can write. After achieving the freedom to write, the major dimensions of success are getting your writing to readers and having those readers find meaning in your words.

Pam: How much do you judge the value of a work by the length of its life?

Bill: You can't always judge the value of a work based on its enduring permanence. I would hope some of my works have a long life, but it's okay if they don't. My favorite plant, the daylilly, has a bloom that is born and dies in one day. Its whole existence is the delivery of this exquisite but transient beauty. Rather than cry about its impending death, it lives fully, reaching for every ray of sun that can spotlight its color. It's okay if my books turn out to be daylillies rather than stone monuments.

Pam: Is there a danger that the writer might become a "personality" and lose part of him- or herself?

Bill: Budd Schulberg once wrote a book called *The Four Seasons of Success* that told how so many writing geniuses—the Steinbecks, the Lewises, the Fitzgeralds—had been destroyed by this American phenomenon of super-success. (I personally think he underestimated the role of their alcohol consumption.) Similar experiences can happen to writers in professional fields. It is this peculiar transformation of the writer into celebrity that can make artists more visible than their art. Some writers have instinctively understood the threat of being turned into a cultural icon. Jean-Paul Sartre, the French existentialist, refused the Nobel Prize in 1964 on the grounds that "writers should not allow themselves to be transformed into institutions."

Pam: I'd like to think it's easier to avoid this if success comes later in life. Do you think that might be the case?

Bill: Yes. I've always thought Joseph Campbell had the best of both worlds. He made such great contributions over such a long period but didn't achieve great cultural visibility until he was in his eighties. He avoided the damaging effects of celebrity status but lived long enough to see his life's work recognized and appreciated by millions of people.

The Curse of Icarus

Pam: How does success threaten the writer?

Bill: I'm becoming very interested in what I think is the risk of success in any profession. I call it the "Curse of Icarus." In Greek mythology, Icarus persuaded his father, Daedalus, to make wings from feathers and wax, which they used to escape their imprisonment within the Labyrinth at Gnossis. Flying from his imprisonment, Icarus became intoxicated with his newfound power. Flying higher and higher towards the sun, the wax of the wings melted, plunging Icarus into the sea. To this day, Icarus is a symbol of the fate of those whose self-intoxication transcends their personal capacities.

I think success draws us toward the sun in ways in which our strengths can be exaggerated into fatal flaws. Fame incites appetites whose insatiability is maddening, like a man whose lust grows in tandem with his declining potency. My personal goal is to slowly and methodically build a body of written work that, while significant in its contribution, escapes the kind of superficial acclimation that would draw me toward the sun.

Pam: Can success also make one a target within one's field?

Bill: There does seem to be a propensity for professional cannibalism in most fields. When someone reaches a certain peak of visibility, it sparks a feeding frenzy from others vying for such visibility. Many of us suffer under the delusion that we are somehow elevated when the celebrated come crashing from their pedestals.

Pam: But aren't we as a culture obsessed with the worship of success?

Bill: I think we like new success. It reinforces the hope for our own future recognition and redemption. What we hate is sustained success, people who—by holding on to their positions of visibility—incite our envy and lust for recognition. If one survives through mid-career, there is a chance one will be again returned to an esteemed position late in one's life. We watch this process unfold at the Oscars and other award ceremonies every year.

Pam: Your image of cannibals is the second reference you've made to people who can harm writers' development.

Bill: There are always people who, having failed to elevate themselves, spend a lifetime attacking people of value and achievement. By tearing them down, they justify and vindicate their own lack of achievement. Ayn Rand's two primary novels—*Fountainhead* and *Atlas Shrugged*—vividly depict characters who try to feed on the strength and creative powers of her book's heroes. Writing success requires that you waste positive energy protecting yourself from such people instead of generating new material. Both aspiring and established writers must beware of leeches who posses an insatiable appetite for the blood of the creative. The writer's social environment can be very influential. My recommendation is to surround yourself with bright, passionate, and positive people and let their chemistry work its magic on you.

Pam: It probably helps to include enough people who are outside the field, who—even if one were highly successful in the field—would never be likely to hear about it, or to care all that much. That gives at least one environment where the writer knows people's reactions are to the person inside, rather than to the writing persona.

I remember that I received a lot of positive feedback after *Breaking the Chain*, the first large work I wrote for PRC. The same thing is happening in stronger terms now that *Increase the Peace* has come out. In each case, when it was time to write my next big document, I found it more difficult to start on it. I was afraid of not measuring up to the earlier work. Is this typical? To what degree does success tend to affect writing productivity?

Bill: Success is paradoxical. On the one hand, success means that your ideas are reaching more people in ways that can have influence. On the other, success can decrease the writer's creativity and writing production. When the experience of success and demands of success take over your consciousness, you are no longer in a process of discovery; you are in a process of defending and promoting and posturing. This is not a new story. The roles of prophet, revolutionary, and artist are often abandoned for the status of celebrity and the role of entertainer. Shamen often get transformed into functionaries within religious hierarchies. People of substance are reduced to gurus of the moment. Passion and experience are reduced to dogma. Messages of substance are corrupted into the spiritual fast food of pop psychology. Success poses dangers for the writer as great as those posed by failure.

Rewards and Costs of the Writing Life

Pam: What's your idea of failure as a writer?

Bill: When our efforts fall short of our hopes and expectations, I think we have to take our disappointment and self-pity and find something useful in the experience. An agency serving addicted women developed a slogan that captured part of its treatment philosophy. The slogan says, "there is no such thing as failure, only feedback." There can be no such thing as a failed writing project, if the writer uses each creative effort as an opportunity for feedback and learning. Monumental successes in writing, as in business, are often built on a foundation of smaller "failures" used as learning experiences.

Pam: What standards do you believe should be used to measure the quality of writing in the field?

Bill: There are a number of standards of excellence to which writers should be held accountable: a command of history; a sensitivity to the diversity of our clients and communities; a capacity for synthesizing numerous disciplines of knowledge; a willingness to tell difficult truths; artistic skill in the presentation of one's message; and the ability to inspire hope.

Pam: What rewards has writing brought to your life?

Bill: Many writers, including myself, are prone to posturing about the pain and torture in writing. What we are less likely to communicate is how much we love it. I think the greatest personal reward is found within the writing process itself, within the experience of creating with words and images.

There are other rewards, too. I've touched people through my written words in ways that would have never been possible if circumstances had pushed writing out of my life. I've achieved professional recognition and monetary rewards. But most of all, I've experienced those intense periods of energized joy when the words gush from me. There are wonderful rewards that come from writing, although some of these come at a price.

Pam: What has that price been in your life?

Bill: Writing demands solitude, self-examination, and a certain level of self-confrontation. It's part of what I like about it. There is in writing a degree of privacy—a dimension of self-intimacy—that I believe is achieved in few other activities or professions. There is a part of every writer that is a loner—who else would choose a vocation that demands such hermit-like self-containment?

But the shadow side of this self-intimacy is the amount of time one is detached from one's physical and social environment. Writers require this capacity for detachment that allows them to shut off everything in the world except the next sentence. It's part of that scatter-brained quality we discussed earlier. Writers need people in their lives who can tolerate such periods of detachment and who don't view the writing desk as a competing friend or lover. The writing obsession consumes time and energy that can cut one off from the mainstream. People are always asking me about this or that aspect of popular culture, and I don't know what they are talking about. If you're reading and writing every day, you've got to be missing some things. Every hour spent within one's own head is an hour not available for acting within the world.

Pam: Where do you think that capacity to detach from the culture comes from?

Bill: I think many writers felt detached long before they began writing. Experiences that create the sense of estrangement and isolation from one's family, neighborhood, and culture enhance this capacity to step outside and observe with an original eye. It's one of the ways painful exclusion or extrusion can become the fuel for creative activity. For some, it's the creative alternative to suicide or homicide.

Competition and Criticism

Pam: Do you see competition among writers within the substance abuse field?

Bill: Yes, as there is in every field. Hemingway and Mailer often used the metaphor of the boxing ring to describe their competition with other writers. While some writers have used competition as a source of motivation to push their writing productivity, I don't think it works that way for me. I consider competition an unhealthy influence on my own writing. When I get caught up in such competition, my attention is diverted outward from the work itself. I end up writing—and usually badly—for the wrong reasons, and I end up reading others not to learn and appreciate, but to judge.

Pam: How do you respond to criticism and critics of your work?

Bill: There aren't a lot of professional critics for what I write and I don't recognize the legitimacy of bystanders to judge my work. The feedback I'm most concerned about is that which comes from my intended audience—people in the trenches of individual and social change. There have been very few occasions when I felt someone in that audience truly misunderstood and inappropriately criticized something I wrote. There are many criticisms and suggestions with which I agree. I'll always have some readers whose thoughts are more incisive than my own. There are also genuine differences of perception or judgement. I try to be as open and non-defensive as possible in the face of criticisms or suggestions. I don't know what my response would be if one of my literary children were viciously attacked. So far, readers say: "What a lovely child, but she would look so much better with a green scarf rather than a red scarf." Put that way, I often agree that green would be a marked improvement.

I think the most damaging critics to the writer are those encountered before the first words are ever written—those critics that through their maliciousness or inadvertent callousness bruise and puncture the creative self. Those critics can haunt us for a lifetime; professional critics are much more expendable.

Changes During Your Writing Career

Pam: What are some of the influences that might prompt one's writing to change over time?

Bill: Maturity and skill refinement can enhance one's writing, just as a loss of passion and changes in physical, emotional and spiritual health can diminish one's writing. I think each writer has a few periods of writing primacy in his or her life. These periods represent a unique synergy between energy, discipline, skill, artistic vision, and writing opportunity. I've wasted time within some of these zones of peak creativity, falsely believing that the state had some permanence. I've let this craving-to-write pass, only to find it gone when I desired its presence. When I feel that zone of creative energy today, I jump into it with the full awareness that it's a special gift that could abandon me at any moment.

Pam: Are there predictable stages of development over the course of a writing career?

Bill: Some writers experience distinct periods, each marked by a shedding of their literary skin, each stage notable by a shift in subject matter or writing medium. I think many writers feel the need to experiment—to move beyond the boundary of their previous work.

Some writers burn themselves out emotionally and lose contact with the source that brings the words. This is not a loss of technical skill but a loss of emotional and spiritual centeredness and connectedness. The process of living and the process of writing must be constantly harmonized.

Pam: What are some of the sources of impetus in your own career that have moved you through your various stages of development?

Bill: There have been some serendipitous collisions with good fortune—meeting certain people or stumbling into opportunities that opened whole new horizons—but I think many of my changes have been launched in reaction to sustained comfort. I've always been suspicious of comfort's power to anesthetize and corrupt. I've always had an irrational fear of getting locked into a situation that would suppress my openness to new challenges. When what

I'm doing begins to develop the musty smell of routine, I jump into something new just to keep the pot stirred up. It has often been a discovery within the new that held the clue to the next stage of my professional development.

Constructing a Writing Career

Pam: What intimidates you as a writer?

Bill: Walking into a large bookstore, staring at thousands of books, and asking myself what difference it will make to write one more book to add to the heap. If I didn't block out the awareness of all those other books, I couldn't write a single word.

Pam: Ah, but just think of the books that have been most valuable to you as a reader. Now think of how many other books had been written on those topics before their authors began them. Aren't you glad they weren't intimidated into silence?

What else is scary for you in approaching a book?

Bill: I'm also intimidated by the prospects of not being read. When a book isn't read, part of the author dies. Authors are dead as long as their books sit confined on a shelf, their binders standing up like cemetery stones, their carefully crafted titles unread epitaphs. Authors come to life in the context of relationship. Life begins each time one of their books is removed from a shelf and its covers are opened. In that sense, my books and I are one. I will have life as long as people keep opening my covers. Writers are intimidated by the prospects of literary death.

Pam: Hmmm. I'm still in awe when people I've just met tell me they've read something I've written.

How does one construct a successful career?

Bill: I think the trick is to focus on constructing a meaningful life rather than on building a successful career. There are a thousand things that can overwhelm us, silence us, crush our spirit, and lead us to embrace hopelessness. My work is my response to those forces, my refusal to give up.

Your question reminds me of a very poignant scene in Alice Walker's book, *Possessing the Secret of Joy*. As the central character Tashi is about to be executed for killing the person who symbolizes the ritualistic and culturally sanctioned genital mutilation of women, her supporters unfurl a banner that answers the book's central question: What is the secret of joy possessed by Black people that has sustained them through tribulation? The banner reads: "<u>RESISTANCE</u> IS THE SECRET OF JOY!" Without hope and vision, people die—emotionally, spiritually, and physically. Great writers like Alice Walker throw us within and beyond ourselves and open up such experiences of hope. They lengthen our memories, extend our vision and dramatize the value of each moment, each decision, each action. Life is about celebrating and resisting. I am blessed because my work has given me rich opportunities for both.

Pam: Do you think there's a cutoff point—an age that you reach, after which it's too hard to begin a discovery process like that? Is it ever too late to start a writing career?

Bill: You begin writing when you can. I didn't write my first book until I was 39 and one of my favorite writers of history, Barbara Tuchman, was fifty when she wrote her first book—and she's won two Pulitzer Prizes.

Chapter 13

Getting Published

The Need for Writers

Pam: What kinds of writers do we need?

Bill: We need all kinds of writers. We need more professional writers to fill the void created by our failure to generate a sustained tradition of clinical literature. We need poets and playwrights and novelists. We need other artists to convey through their various artistic mediums the realities of addiction and the hope of recovery. We need many mediums to educate and to celebrate who and what we are.

Exploring New Territory

Pam: We've hoped through these dialogues to recruit and inspire a new generation of writers within the field. Where should these writers begin?

Bill: I think they have to seek out the larger stories within which their personal story can unfold. I think they have to seek out opportunities to participate in the turning points of our professional and cultural history. You have to find issues that are culturally and personally important and find a way to become a positive part of this evolving story. Whether the story is AIDS or violence or sexual abuse, you have to find a way in which your ability to put words on paper can serve as a healing force.

Pam: What writing territory is open for exploration?

Bill: The territory is limited only by one's interests, imagination, and willingness to endure in the search. There are areas of critical need that I think will demand the attention of many writers during the coming years.

Pam: What are some of these areas in the substance abuse treatment field?

Bill: I think a beginning place is to chart the territory we have extensively explored during the past decade. The explosive growth of the treatment system brought thousands of fresh eyes and ears and minds into the field. We have to document the best of what was seen, heard and thought during the decade. We need to document our core knowledge and core skills so that they can become the foundation for our next surge into the future. Without such documentation, we are in danger of losing the best within our past and current practices as we move forward. There are dangers that this core knowledge could be lost in the current restructuring of how substance abuse treatment services are organized and funded. We need to document the detailed nuances of our mainstream and cutting edge treatment and prevention models.

Pam: What new territory is open for exploration beyond the mainstream?

Bill: I think the last decade of research on "special populations" has stretched the traditional single-pathway model of addiction treatment to its breaking point. So much of what we know about addiction in this country is based on our experience with Anglo, male, "Gamma species" alcoholics. Beginning breakthroughs in research with women, adolescents, people of color, and people with concurrent substance abuse and psychiatric impairment—to name a few—have created a need for a multiple-pathway model of addiction and recovery. While some writers are documenting the mainstream technology of the field, others need to discover for whom this technology doesn't work and what new technology is needed. I think the next decade will bring a dramatic broadening of our conceptualization of the etiology of various substance abuse disorders and the variable pathways through which people recover. We need writers with the courage to observe and tell the truth about what they see, even if these truths challenge our historical explanations of addiction and our approaches to prevention and treatment.

Pam: I agree, but it's also important not to dismiss the usefulness of an entire technology for all members of a particular gender or ethnicity, if it's working well for some. In some cases it might be better to pull the technology apart and look at what elements are and aren't working for whom, and why. And from what I've heard about the non-confrontational approaches that seem to work better with women, adolescents, people of color, etc., I wouldn't be surprised if they also proved more effective with European-American men.

What kinds of writing will help us understand the diversity of substance abuse patterns without settling on simplistic answers?

Bill: We need to apply our best analytical and scientific thinking to our understanding of people whose needs are different than culturally empowered alcoholic men, but we need non-analytic approaches of understanding as well. We need literature that enhances our experiential understanding of and empathic identification with these clients. We need our front-line treatment and prevention workers to begin constructing tales that celebrate the resilience and strength of individuals, families and communities.

Pam: Describe what this literature might look like.

Bill: There has emerged a new genre through which the stories of "patients" with serious disorders are told in a fundamentally new way. Irving Yalom's work, *Love's Executioner*, and Susan Baur's, *The Dinosaur Man*, have recently sought to humanize people with psychiatric illness through their "clinical tales." I think the real pioneer of this genre was Oliver Sacks. His book of clinical tales of various neurological disorders, *The Man Who Mistook His Wife for a Hat*, is one of the most sensitively written works I've ever read. It describes how illness is experienced from the inside rather than in the cold, jargon-filled language of science. Someone needs to humanize the diverse range of addictive disorders in the same manner that Oliver Sacks humanized neurological disorders. We need our front-line clinicians to begin constructing their own clinical tales—tales that respectfully tell the diverse stories of those addicted and those recovering.

Writing as a Tool in Prevention and Treatment

Pam: One thing we haven't touched on in our discussions is the potential use of writing as a clinical technique in addiction treatment, or as a tool in prevention. What are your thoughts about using writing in these contexts?

Bill: We have used what we call "bibliotherapy"—reading assignments that are interpreted for personal applicability—extensively within substance abuse prevention and treatment, but writing remains an underutilized tool of personal transformation.

"Breaking silence" and "discovering one's voice" are important themes in a survivalist literature that has filled thousands of library shelves. For the survivor, calling forth memory is an act of both personal and political significance. Through writing, one can personally heal and take action to prevent the victimization of others. This is particularly apparent in the Holocaust literature. It's as if the survivors said: "We will write to exorcise our own demonic memories and, in doing so, we will create a body of literature of such volume and vividness that the world will never be able to erase these events from its history." I think there is a parallel literature emerging on the victimization of women and children around the world.

Journaling and structured writing experiences can be effectively used to facilitate self-discovery, self-healing and social change. While writing is increasingly being explored as a medium of personal healing, I know of few sustained efforts to explore writing as a medium for prevention. I think there would be great potential for such experiments.

Pam: Are there any resources that would be particularly helpful to someone interested in writing for self-discovery or self-healing?

Bill: Richard Solly and Roseann Lloyd wrote a wonderful little book entitled *Journey Notes* that is all about how to use writing as a tool in personal recovery.

Pam: What do you think are some of the "big stories" that have yet to be written?

Bill: As I noted earlier, I think the big story right now is the loss of community. There are key elements within this big story that have yet to be fully told. Many of us need to create stories that can explain the origins and legacies of the violence of the last decade. We need to tell how the jail and the prison have emerged as dominant and imposed institutions within poor communities and communities of color since the 1980s. We need to describe even more specifically the forces through which drug cultures and prison cultures are replacing the family, the church, the school, and the workplace as agents of socialization. We need to forge a literature that can help us understand how our institutions are evolving.

Pam: What about the state of human services themselves? Shouldn't we be writing papers that assess where we are and push us forward?

Bill: I think we are at a critical turning point in the evolution of human service agencies. Such agencies have a long history in this culture, but they grew dramatically during the past two decades, becoming highly institutionalized in our structures and processes. There are many organizations decaying from within. There are likely to be increasing numbers of people suggesting that if the human service system isn't re-energized and revolutionized, it should be abandoned. It's more a middle-class welfare system than it is a medium of personal or social transformation. It's becoming a jobs program for the middle class whose role is containment and pacification of people, cultures, and communities being discarded by this society. It's becoming a salve through which the consciences of the empowered are anesthetized into the belief that they have done their "fair share." Professional helpers are becoming paid substitutes for family and friends. Their role is to fill gaps in a disintegrating social tissue and serve as a buffer between the empowered and the disempowered. Human service agencies need to recapture their role as agents of change.

Pam: What role can writers play in this renewal process?

Bill: The writer's job is to bring us our worst and our best. Writers can hold a mirror up which in the brightness of their language reveals all of our personal and collective blemishes. Writers can also find and celebrate pockets of hope—to show what old and new values look like in action. Our function is to confront, inform, and inspire. Our function is to help us individually and collectively to break out of passivity.

The Experience of Being Published

Pam: What do you like best about being published?

Bill: The knowledge that somewhere, someone is reading one of my books at this moment. There are only so many people you can touch face-to-face in your lifetime. Getting published is a way to extend the range of your touch.

Pam: What's it like for you to see your books in a bookstore or to have people ask you to sign one of your books?

Bill: It's wonderful. Signing books was really embarrassing for me at first because it felt pretentious—that self-consciousness I talked about earlier. Today, I consider it a privilege. It's a way of personalizing the relationship between myself and the reader that I was striving for when I sat down to write the book.

Tips on Getting Published

Pam: Do you have any suggestions for the aspiring writer who's trying to get published in the field?

Bill: I think the first focus should be on refining one's craft and creating a body of publishable work. I can promise new writers that they will be very happy in retrospect that some of their early work didn't get published. I recently ran across one of my earliest professional papers. My lack of understanding of the subject of this paper was matched only by the intensity with which I attacked it.   Rarely have I ever demonstrated my ignorance with such clarity and enthusiasm. Thank God some of this work wasn't published!

As you begin to create a body of work, you have to get your work to readers however you can. Copy and distribute papers to key people. Find newsletters that will publish short articles. Submit bits and fragments wherever you can. Approach established authors with offers to collaborate with research and writing assistance on any of their projects. The key is to begin to build a list of published work, no matter how humble. You must get your words to your readers through whatever mechanism you can discover or invent.

I may not know as many of these sources as other writers in the field because so much of my writing is published through the Institute.

Pam: What considerations went into your decision to have your work published through the Institute?

Bill: There was a wonderful confluence of interests. The Lighthouse Institute was wanting quality work to launch their involvement in publishing within the addictions field, and I was looking for a publisher who would ensure me a substantial amount of artistic freedom. People often say to me that I could sell a lot more books or make a lot of money if I went through a major publisher, and if those were my goals, I would probably do that. But I would rather have 10,000 people read a book I wrote than 100,000 read a book of mine whose essential character was violated to make it attractive to a broader commercial audience. Many authors have had such works mutilated and diluted ("edited") for the mainstream literature of pop psychology.

While there are some disadvantages—such as limited circulation—in having my work published through the Institute, there are some real benefits. I don't have to worry about my work being evaluated by someone who knows nothing about my field and the people for whom I'm writing. When I present five potential writing projects within the Institute, each is evaluated first and foremost based on its potential contribution to the field.

This whole series of publications (the Conversation Series), for example, was viewed as a way to highlight specialty roles and skills within the field—to celebrate the unique contributions of writers, trainers, researchers and others with specialty niches. These publications are not likely to make a huge profit, but they may fire the imagination of some workers to explore these areas as potential career moves. I like the freedom to move into areas of need that may not be commercially attractive to mainstream publishers. At the Institute, the weight is on the import of the topic. If the project proposal is approved, I know my work on it will go to press.

Pam: Does that mean that you won't work with major publishers?

Bill: It means that I would only work with a commercial publisher if I were coming from a position of strength. I don't write books for the mainstream public, and it would alter the nature of what I do to transform what I write for professionals into self-help pablum which a publisher could use to feed this culture's current appetite for the spiritual equivalent of fast food. Once the commercial success of my work—as I wrote it—has been established, the Institute may re-release some of my work through a mainstream publisher. With that success as a base, we are much less likely to have to alter the basic character of the work.

Pam: That makes sense, but let me say a few words in defense of the "spiritual fast food pablum of pop psychology." I'm sure there are many examples of low quality, rampant excess, and superfluity in the realm of self-help literature. But I'm equally sure that there are millions of people who simply don't have access to other kinds of help—or don't believe they have access, which amounts to the same thing. If a book—or even a TV show—that I consider simplistic can catalyze positive change in people's lives, do I have any right to look down on it just because the same concepts have been presented more intelligently elsewhere? Until I can come up with a substitute that's acceptable to that audience, I don't think so.

That's enough soapbox for me. Would you advise other writers to avoid mainstream publishers too?

Bill: I would say "be cautious with" rather than "avoid." Few writers have access to a single outlet for their work as I have at the Institute. For writers who are writing for the general public, I would recommend both mainstream commercial publishers and the growing number of small presses around the country who publish titles in various specialty areas. My only caution in working with publishers is to make sure the book that comes out is the book you had in your heart when you began writing—make sure it's the book you want your name on.

Pam: What about writing on contract?

Bill: Some writers are contracted to write certain topical pieces. For example a writer might sign a contract that he or she will write a 5,000-word article on substance abuse in the workplace for a fee of $1,000. In this type of writing, the writer has a publisher before the first word is ever written.

Pam: What agencies are most likely to contract for this kind of writing?

Bill: The professional writer with expertise in the substance abuse field who wishes to write contractually should contact those agencies who are involved in contractual service work with state and federal substance abuse agencies and allied agencies that are involved in substance abuse issues. These firms provide contractual services in research, evaluation, training, technical assistance, curriculum development, and policy analysis. Nearly all contractual work includes written products, and writing skills are highly sought after by such contractors. Lists of contractors may be obtained from these agencies.

Pam: Do you have any advice on getting articles published?

Bill: I recommend beginning with short topical pieces that can be published in quarterly publications of professional associations or other local or regional publications within the field. These provide opportunities to break into print and provide rehearsal for submitting more substantive articles to the major professional journals.

We talked earlier about knowing your audience. The best advice I can give is to know your journals. Subscribe to the major journals and get to know the kinds of articles each prefers. Note for each the normal length, the preferred topics, the tone, the writing style, and the format.

Pam: What journals would be good ones for aspiring writers to consider as potential publishers?

Bill: I think the best strategy for journal selection is to visit a library, such as the Prevention First library, that carries most of the major prevention and treatment journals and review which of these carries articles closest to the one you are writing. By regularly reviewing these journals, you will develop an instinct about which article to submit to which journal.

Pam: Can an article be submitted to more than one journal at a time?

Bill: Historically, writing ethics and etiquette called for submission of a work to only one publisher at a time, but this is changing somewhat. Nearly all journals will send you their guidelines for authors which detail their submission requirements. These guidelines identify whether the journal demands exclusive submission or allows simultaneous submission of articles.

Pam: What are the first steps in finding a book publisher?

Bill: There aren't hard and fast rules in this area. Perhaps the most frequent submission format is a detailed outline with a sample chapter. Some authors submit completed works. The best advice I have on selecting a publisher is to choose one who has published works that you like and respect. The requirements for submission for particular publishers can be found in such books as *Writer's Market* or in such journals as *Writer's Digest.*

Pam: What effect do you see the current economic difficulties—particularly in the substance abuse field—having on the prospect of book publishing?

Bill: I think we will see a decline in the number of self-help books catering to a recovering audience, but there continues to be a vacuum in the area of well written, highly practical treatment texts. I think there will continue to be a market for state-of-the-art treatment and prevention texts during the next decade.

Pam: How does the writer protect his or her work?

Bill: I'm pretty loose with most of my writing. I don't think I've ever denied anyone permission to use or reprint parts of my work. I consider benign theft of my work a form of flattery and am satisfied if the ideas get out—after all, that was my primary reason for writing to begin with. There is a kind of malignant theft that I do detest. That is when someone takes my work and claims it as their own or seeks to sell my work without my permission. I copyright most of my major papers and books explicitly to protect myself from this latter form of piracy.

Writing Mottoes

Pam: You've referred to a number of mottoes that are part of your writing "creed." Could you summarize them here? They might make a fitting closing to our discussions.

Bill: The ideas, and many of the phrases, embedded within these mottoes are not my original creations, and yet each has a highly personalized meaning that shapes a separate dimension of my own writing psychology. The mottoes posted over my writing desk are the following:

Do What Matters! (B. Fuller)
Follow Your Bliss! (J. Campbell)
Honor the Source!
Eulogize the Living! (R. Furey)
Do Your Homework!
Respect Your Reader!
Break Silence!
Tell the Truth! Then tell the hidden truth!
If you write it, you must live it!
Dig deep; Reach Wide!
Flow, Not Force!
Minimize Theory; Maximize Detail!
Rise Above!
Leap and the Net Will Appear! (J. Cameron)
Keep Your Eyes on the Prize! (civil rights slogan)
Pace yourself! Remember, it's a marathon!

When I'm unhappy with one of my creations, it's usually because I've failed to adhere to one or more elements of this writing creed.

Pam: Do you have any final comments to address to our readers?

Bill: Perhaps a closing invitation. There are many "shadow artists" in our field—people who have enormous creative energy and latent skills but who have been afraid to step into the light. The current needs of the field provide an opportunity and a duty for such people to step forward to help shape our future. If you are one of these shadow artists, it's time to jump into the fray. We need you!

Bibliography

Achebe, C. (1989). *Hopes and Impediments.* New York: Anchor Books.

Adler, M. (1972). *How to Read a Book.* New York: Simon and Schuster.

Allen, W., Ed., (1988). *Conversations with Kurt Vonnegut.* Jackson, MS: University Press of Mississippi.

Asimov, J. and I. Asimov (1987). *How to Enjoy Writing.* New York: Walker and Company.

Bateson, M. (1990). *Composing a Life.* New York: Penguin Books.

Baur, S. (1991). *The Dinosaur Man.* New York: HarperCollins Publishers.

Becker, H. (1986). *Writing for Social Scientists.* Chicago: University of Chicago Press.

Bernstein, T. (1965). *The Careful Writer.* New York: McMillan.

Bissel, L. and Royce, J. (1987). *Ethics for Addiction Professionals.* Center City, MN: Hazelden.

Bruccoli, M. (1986). *Conversations with Ernest Hemingway.* Jackson, MS: University Press of Mississippi.

Burroughs, W. (1953). *Junkie.* New York: Ace Books.

Burroughs, W. (1959). *Naked Lunch.* New York: Grove Weidenfeld.

Cameron, J. (1992). *The Artist's Way.* New York: Jeremy P. Tarcher/Perigee Books.

Campbell, J. (1988). *The Power of Myth.* New York: Doubleday.

232

Cohen, S. (1988). *The Chemical Brain: The Neurochemistry of Addictive Disorders.* Irvine, CA: Care Institute.

Csikszentmihalyi, M. (1990). *Flow: The Psychology of Oprimal Experience.* New York: Harper and Row.

Dardis, T. (1989). *The Thirsty Muse.* Boston, MA: Houghton Mifflin Company.

Dillard, A. (1989). *The Writing Life.* New York: HarperCollins Publishers.

Einstein, A. Quoted in Safransky, S. (1990). *Sunbeams: A Book of Quotations.* Berkeley, CA: North Atlantic Books.

Elbow, P. (1981). *Writing with Power.* New York: Oxford University Press.

Elliot, J. (1989). *Conversations with Maya Angelou.* Jackson, MS: University Press of Mississippi.

Fiore, N. (1989). *The Now Habit.* Los Angeles: Jeremy P. Tarcher, Inc.

Foote, S. (1989). *Conversations with Shelby Foote.* Jackson, MS: University Press of Mississippi.

Furey, R. (1993). *The Joy of Kindness.* New York: Crossroad Publishing Company.

Gardner, H. (1993). *Creating Minds: An Anatomy of Creativity Seen Through the Lives of Freud, Einstein, Picasso, Stravinsky, Elliot, Graham, and Gandhi.* New York: BasicBooks.

Gluck, L. (1991). The Education of the Poet, in Shelnutt, E., *The Confidence Woman.* Marietta, GA: Longstreet Publishing Company.

Goodwin, D. (1988). *Alcohol and the Writer.* New York: Penguin Books.

Heilbrun, C. (1988). *Writing A Woman's Life.* New York: Ballantine Books

Hinz, E., Ed., (1975). *A Woman Speaks: The Lectures, Seminars, and Interviews of Anaïs Nin*. Athens, OH: Ohio University Press.

Hodgkinson, H. (1991). Reform versus reality. *Phi Delta Kappan*, September, pp 9-16.

Jamison, K. R. (1993). *Touched with Fire: Manic-Depressive Illness and the Artistic Temperament*. New York: The Free Press.

Jeffers, S. (1987). *Feel the Fear and Do it Anyway*. New York: Fawcet Columbine.

Kasl, C. (1992). *Many Roads, One Journey*. New York: HarperCollins Publishers.

Kurtz, E. (1979). *Not God: A History of Alcoholics Anonymous*. Center City, MN: Hazelden.

Kurtz, E. and Ketcham, K. (1992). *The Spirituality of Imperfection*. New York: Bantam Books.

Lawrence, J. and Lee, R. (1989). Interviewed in *On Being A Writer*, ed. by Strickland, B. Cincinnati, OH: Writer's Digest Books.

Levin, J. (1990). *Alcoholism: A Biopsychosocial Approach*. New York: Hemisphere Publishing Company.

Malcolm X with Haley, A. (1965). *The Autobiography of Malcolm X*. New York: Grove Press.

McKnight, R. (1992). If You Don't Know Me By Now, in Shelnutt, E. *My Poor Elephant*. Atlanta, GA: Longstreet Press.

Miller, H. (1964). *Henry Miller on Writing*. New York: New Directions Publishing Company.

Musto, D. (1973). *The American Disease*. New Haven: Yale University Press.

234

Nin, A. (1975). *The Diary of Anaïs Nin.* San Diego: Harcourt, Brace, & Co.

Polking, K. (1987). *The Beginning Writer's Answer Book.* Cincinnati, OH: Writer's Digest Books.

Prather, H. (1977). *Notes on Love and Courage.* New York: Doubleday.

Prevention Resource Center (1991). *Breaking the Chain: Making Prevention Programs Work for Children of Addicted Families.* Springfield, IL: Prevention Resource Center, Inc.

Prevention Resource Center (1994). *Increase the Peace: A Primer on Fear, Violence, and Transformation.* Springfield, IL: Prevention Resource Center, Inc.

Prevention Resource Center (1994). *Learning to Listen, Learning to Heal: A Modular Training Series on Addiction, Recovery, and Prevention.* Springfield, IL: Prevention Resource Center, Inc.

Prevention Resource Center (1991). *Tools for Transformation: A community Empowerment Approach to Reclaiming Cultural Traditions.* Springfield, IL: Prevention Resource Center, Inc.

Rand, A. (1986). *The Fountainhead.* New York: Macmillan Publishers.

Rand, A. (1957). *Atlas Shrugged.* New York: Random House.

Rubin, L. (1983). *Intimater Strangers: Men and Women Together.* New York: Harper & Row.

Sacks, O. (1985). *The Man Who Mistook His Wife for a Hat.* New York: Harper and Row Publishers.

Shaughnessy, S. (1993). *Walking on Alligators.* New York: HarperCollins Publishers.

Seabrook, W. (1947). *Asylum.* New York: Bantam Books.

Schulberg, B. (1983). *Writers in America: The Four Seasons of Success.* New York: Stein and Day Publishers.

Schweitzer, A. (1933). *Out of My Life and Thought.* New York: Henry Holt and Company.

Schweitzer, A. quoted in Safransky, S. (1990). *Sunbeams: A Book of Quotations.* Berkeley, CA: North Atlantic Books.

Siegal, R. (1989). *Intoxication.* New York: E.P. Dutton.

Solly, R. and Lloyd, R. (1989). *Journey Notes: Writing for Recovery and Spiritual Growth.* San Francisco: Harper/Hazelden.

Standley, F. and Pratt, L., Ed., (1989). *Conversations with James Baldwin.* Jackson, MS: University Press of Mississippi.

Steinbeck, J. (1989). *Working Days: The Journals of The Grapes of Wrath,* edited by Demott, R. New York: Viking Press.

Sternburg, J. (1980). *The Writer on Her Work.* New York: W.W. Norton & Company.

Strunk, and White, (1979). *The Elements of Style.* New York: Macmillan Publishers.

Tavris, C. (1992). *The Mismeasure of Woman.* New York: Simon and Schuster.

Thoreau, H. (1989). *Thoreau on Writing.* Conway, Arkansas: University of Central Arkansas Press.

Tillich, P. (1966). *On the Boundary: An Autobiographical Sketch.* New York: Charles Scribner's Sons.

Walker, A. (1992). *Possessing the Secret of Joy.* New York: Harcourt Brace Jovanovich.

White, E.B. (1990). *Writings From the New Yorker: 1927-1976*. New York: HarperCollins Publishers.

White, W. (1986). *Incest in the Organizational Family: The Ecology of Burnout in Closed Systems*. Bloomington, IL: Lighthouse Institute.

White, W. (1990). *The Culture of Addiction, The Culture of Recovery* Bloomington, IL: Lighthouse Institute.

White, W. (1993). *Critical Incidents: Ethical Issues in Substance Abuse Prevention and Treatment*. Bloomington, IL: Lighthouse Institute.

White, W. and Chaney, R. (1993). *Metaphors of Transformation: Feminine and Masculine*. Bloomington, IL: Lighthouse Institute.

White, W., Joleaud, B, Dudek, F., and Carty, B. (1994). *The Training Life*. Bloomington, IL: Lighthouse Institute

White, W. (1994). *Voices of Survival, Voices of Service*. Chicago, IL: The AIDS Foundation of Chicago.

Williams, C. with Laird, R. (1992). *No Hiding Place*. New York: Harper Collins.

Woll, P. and Gorski, T. (1995). *Worth Protecting: Women, Men, and Freedom from Sexual Aggression*. Independence, Missouri: Herald House/Independence Press.

Woll, P., Schmidt, M. and Heinemann, A. (1993). *Alcohol and Other Drug Abuse Prevention for People With Traumatic Brain and Spinal Cord Injuries*. Chicago, IL: Midwest Regional Head Injury Center for Rehabilitation and Prevention.

Woolf, V. (1929). *A Room of One's Own*. New York: Harcourt Brace Jovanovich, Inc.

Worthington, M. (1966). *The Strange World of Willie Seabrook.* New York: Harcourt, Brace, & World , Inc.

Yalom, I. (1989). *Love's Executioner.* New York: Basic Books, Inc.